Our Day to End Poverty

24 Ways You Can Make a Difference

Shannon Daley-Harris and Jeffrey Keenan

with Karen Speerstra

Berrett-Koehler P

San Fra

a BK Cur

Berrett-Koehler Publishers, Inc.
235 Montgomery Street, Suite 650
San Francisco, CA 94104-2916
Tel: (415) 288-0260 Fax: (415) 362-2512 www.bkconnection.com

Ordering Information
Quantity sales. Special discounts are available on quantity purchases by corporations, associations, and others. For details, contact the "Special Sales Department" at the Berrett-Koehler address above.

Individual sales. Berrett-Koehler publications are available through most bookstores. They can also be ordered directly from Berrett-Koehler: Tel: (800) 929-2929; Fax: (802) 864-7626; www.bkconnection.com.

Orders for college textbook/course adoption use. Please contact Berrett-Koehler: Tel: (800) 929-2929; Fax: (802) 864-7626.

Orders by U.S. trade bookstores and wholesalers. Please contact Ingram Publisher Services, Tel: (800) 509-4887; Fax: (800) 838-1149; E-mail: customer.service@ingrampublisherservices.com; or visit www.ingrampublisherservices.com/Ordering for details about electronic ordering.

Printed in the United States of America

Berrett-Koehler books are printed on long-lasting acid-free paper. When it is available, we choose paper that has been manufactured by environmentally responsible processes. These may include using trees grown in sustainable forests, incorporating recycled paper, minimizing chlorine in bleaching, or recycling the energy produced at the paper mill.

Library of Congress Cataloging-in-Publication Data

Daley-Harris, Shannon.
Our day to end poverty : 24 ways you can make a difference / Shannon Daley-Harris and Jeffrey Keenan, with Karen Speerstra.
p. cm.
Includes bibliographical references and index.
ISBN 978-1-57675-446-7 (pbk. : alk. paper)
1. Poverty. 2. Social action. I. Keenan, Jeffrey, 1961– II. Speerstra, Karen. III. Title.

HC79.P6D35 2007
362.5'574—dc22
2007009063

12 11 10 09 08 07 10 9 8 7 6 5 4 3 2 1

Cover photograph: Stockbyte/Getty Images. Cover design by PemaStudio.
Interior design and composition by Gary Palmatier, Ideas to Images.
Elizabeth von Radics, copyeditor; Mike Mollett, proofreader; Medea Minnich, indexer.

Dedication

To our children, Micah, Sophie, Ted, Gabe, Meghan, Mollie, Destiny, Jefferson, Joel, Nathan, Julia, and Schuyler, and children all around the world, with hope and determination that they will one day wake up in a world without poverty.

Contents

Preface

Not long ago the *New York Times* ran a front-page article about child labor as seen through the eyes of a six-year-old African indentured servant. He lives far from his family and is roused from a dirt floor to work long, hard hours, dragging a heavy wooden oar nearly his own weight and paddling and bailing out the leaky fishing boat of his master, who deals out beatings but little food. I thought about every six-year-old I knew when, out of earshot of his master, the little boy whispered to the reporter, "I don't like it here."

What was equally powerful was the response to the article, as readers wrote to the *Times* and expressed their frustration that the article didn't tell them what they could do to help. Wrote one reader who wept over the article, "There are moments when there is value in simply feeling the deep pain of another's situation. But in an age when most of us...already feel powerless about what happens in the world, a little bit of guidance toward action—anything to hang on to—would have been both kind and potentially helpful for all." *Our Day to End Poverty: 24 Ways You Can Make a Difference* is a book for all of us who know that there is poverty and suffering in our world and who *want to know what we can do* to help. This isn't a book to convince you to care about global poverty—we trust that you already do. This is a book for those of us who have felt hopeless or helpless—a book to show what each of us can do to make a difference.

Our Day to End Poverty invites us to look at every day and begin thinking about poverty in new and creative ways. Inspired by the landmark bestseller *50 Simple Things You Can Do to Save the Earth*, this book offers scores of practical, doable (although not always simple) actions anyone can take to help eliminate poverty.

Each chapter helps connect our daily experiences to those of people around the world. Most of us begin our day by eating breakfast—so the first chapter focuses on addressing world hunger. We might then take the kids to school—what can we do to help make education available to all? In the afternoon we tackle our e-mail correspondence or text-message our friends—how can we ensure access to appropriate technology that can become a route out of poverty? In the evening we brush our teeth and fill a glass with water—what can we do so that everyone has access to clean water?

In the year 2000, world leaders met and committed to eight United Nations (UN) Millennium Development Goals to end poverty in our lifetime and to cut extreme hunger and poverty in half by 2015, along with other key progress on poverty-related problems. The twenty-four chapters in this book show how each of us can contribute to these ambitious but achievable goals to improve the lives of people around the world.

These chapters look at a range of poverty-related issues both in the United States and worldwide, balancing what we can do at home and what we can do farther away. This isn't an either/or, us-and-them problem. This is about all of us because we are all in this together. We live together on one planet, and what affects our brothers and sisters in one region affects us all.

You can read this book straight through, as though we're spending one long day together, starting in the morning and ending at night. Or start with a topic you care deeply about, whether it's hunger, education, or health care. Maybe you'll just pick up the book and flip it open to see what difference you could make that day. It is written so that each chapter can stand alone, chock-full of actions you can take to learn more, contribute, serve, and make changes in the way you live.

You may already be wondering, *Am I supposed to be taking an action every hour of every day? How could I possibly do all these actions? I'm overwhelmed!* Don't worry; you aren't expected to do something every hour or even every day. That's why there are so many choices: so you can choose what is right for you and your life.

You can do some of these actions on your own, or you can team up with other people. It's up to you. One action today may lead to other actions tomorrow. This is a step-by-step process. Who knows where it will lead?

In the words of Marian Wright Edelman, founder and president of the Children's Defense Fund, "If you don't like the way the world is, you change it. You have an obligation to change it. You just do it one step at a time."

Will we? Nelson Mandela, referring to the UN Millennium Development Goals, said, "Sometimes it falls upon a generation to be great. You can be that great generation."

If we rise to the challenge, working together, one day six-year-olds across our globe may declare aloud, "I like it here."

Acknowledgments

Publishing a book is an inherently collaborative effort. *Our Day to End Poverty: 24 Ways You Can Make a Difference* has been especially so. Although I (Shannon) was the writer, the book was conceived by Jeff Keenan and Joy Anderson, who is the president and founder of Criterion Ventures; it was enriched by Karen Speerstra's writing, editing, and publishing experience and strengthened by the insights and recommendations of Jackie VanderBrug, Criterion's managing director.

Joy and Jackie were invaluable members of the book team; it would not exist without them. Their experience in managing dynamic team processes, their network of cool people doing important work, and their big vision and probing insights were integral to the book's development. Sarah Ruberti, Criterion Ventures' traffic manager, assumed the monumental task of sending draft chapters to dozens of reviewers and returning their responses to me. We owe much to her diligence and organizational skills.

On a personal note, I offer my deepest thanks to my husband, Sam Daley-Harris, for his own inspiring work to end poverty and his insights, support, and contacts, which strengthened this book immeasurably. I'm grateful for support from Eliot, Patti, and Jad Daley and Serena Schorr. Deep thanks to Marian Wright Edelman for her work to end child poverty in our rich nation and the opportunity to serve with her in that mission for nearly twenty years. I appreciate the input from Macky Alston, Linda Gerard, Lisey Good, Jen Klein, Liz McCloskey, and Alison and Campbell Stevenson. My thanks also to Elizabeth, Paul, Gabriel, and others at Port City Java, whose warm welcome and iced coffee sustained me throughout more than a year of writing!

Jeff expresses grateful appreciation to his family for their incredible patience and support throughout the time it took to bring this book to completion. Thanks to John Sage, Nancy Lewis, and Te Davis and to the 2006 Criterion Convergence attendees for their reviews of early drafts. Thanks also to Maria Finch and Victor Meiusi for their input on the structure of the book and its chapters. For their input on the title, cover, and/or book structure, thanks to Jacque Mahan, Leslie Piacitelli, Julia Dowd, and Debi, Meghan, Edith, and Jerry Keenan. Erick Goss and Suparna Bhasin provided valuable publishing guidance, and personal thanks go to James Dailey for his chapter review. Finally, thanks to the many friends who took the time to read a chapter or two and offer feedback from a reader's perspective.

Karen extends her appreciation to Barry Childs for providing information on Africa Bridge and its work on fighting AIDS and supporting AIDS orphans. And thanks go to Ellen Frost, Penny and Joe Hauser, Carol Frenier, Judy Walke, Jan Field, Julia Blackbourn, and Joel and John Speerstra for feedback on title choices and organizational issues.

We would not have had the audacity to tackle such an enormous subject without knowing that there were many wise, experienced, and insightful people to whom we could turn to review and improve each chapter. For generously giving their time for thoughtful review, sharing their unique and important perspectives and experiences, and most especially for the work that they are doing day in and day out to end poverty, we offer our deepest appreciation. To be sure, any errors and omissions that remain are our responsibility.

Mary Baich, president, Vesper Society

David Beckmann, president, Bread for the World

Jeremy Ben-Ami, senior vice president, Fenton Communications

Bob Berg, international consultant

Gary Bolles, president and co-founder, Microcast Communications

Kolleen Bouchane, Global Education for All Campaign manager, RESULTS Educational Fund

Midge Bowman, Frye Art Museum

Alison Buist, director, Health Division, Children's Defense Fund

Laura Cassell, chief executive officer, Catholic Charities of the Diocese of Rockville Centre

Margaret Catley-Carlson, chair, Global Water Partnership

Maya Chorengel, president and managing director, Dignity Fund

Kathleen Close, president, Microbusiness USA

Sig Cohen

Steve Commins, lecturer, UCLA

Alex Counts, president, Grameen Foundation

James Dailey, technical project manager, Grameen Technology Center

Tim Dearborn, associate director, World Vision International

Jim Diers, community builder

Meredith Dodson, director of domestic campaigns, RESULTS

Martha Dolben, chair, African Food and Peace Foundation

Susan Dorazio, teacher, Nonotuck Community School

Jonah Edelman, executive director, Stand for Children

Robert Egger, president, D.C. Central Kitchen

Pamela Frank, vice president, Best Doctors

Timothy Freundlich, director of strategic development, Calvert Foundation

Bob Friedman, general counsel, Corporation for Enterprise Development

Elizabeth Glenshaw, director of CI market and industry development, Calvert Social Investment Foundation

John Graham, president, The Giraffe Project

Danny Grossman, founder and chief executive officer, Wild Planet

Kate Guedj, vice president for philanthropic and donor services, The Boston Foundation

Jenny Hannibal, director of external affairs, Village Reach

Paulette Hardin, executive director, SHARE

Ronne Hartfield, international consultant, Museum Education and Planning

John Hatch, founder, FINCA International

Jean Hazell, Harvard Business School

Pam Horowitz

John Ivanoski, partner, KPMG

Peter Johnson, partner, Development World Markets

Mary Jo Larson, principal, Symmetry International Associates

Michele Lerner, writer, Bread for the World

Jonathan Lewis, managing chair, MicroCredit Enterprises

Michael Melendez, associate professor, Simmons College School of Social Work

Calvin Miller, senior rural finance officer, UN Food and Agriculture Organization

Scott Morris, executive director, Memphis Church Health Center

Emily Nichols, communications and media manager, International Justice Mission

Warren Radtke, consultant, Business Advice and Counsel

Jill Schumann, chief executive officer, Lutheran Services in America

Brian Sellers Peterson, director of West Coast operations, Episcopal Relief and Development

Arloc Sherman, senior researcher, Center for Budget and Policy Priorities

Paul Shoemaker, executive director, Social Venture Partners Seattle

Melah Skoll, partner, manager, and consultant, Soul of Money Institute

Melissa Snow, deputy director of communications, Shared Hope International

Laura Stein, program associate, New Visions for Public Schools

Sally Stoeker, lead researcher, Shared Hope International

Kimberlea Tracey, New England regional director, U.S. Fund for UNICEF

Mike Troutman, strategic development internal consultant, ELCA Board of Pensions

Lynne Twist, founder, Soul of Money Institute

Susan Wefald, vice president, program, Ms. Foundation for Women, Inc.

Lisa Witter, executive vice president and general manager, Fenton Communications

We had hoped to find a publisher who would take a collaborative approach to our book, and Berrett-Koehler has far exceeded our expectations. We appreciate Steve Piersanti's enthusiastic response to the concept when Joy first described it to him. Jeevan Sivasubramaniam has provided steady oversight, and Ken Lupoff headed up an outstanding team.

Elizabeth von Radics's skilled and thorough editing greatly strengthened the book, and we appreciate Gary Palmatier's terrific design.

Finally, we thank and acknowledge all of the heroes, named and unnamed, who work every day for the end of poverty in their own lives, our communities, and the world. We thank our world leaders who had the foresight to create the UN Millennium Development Goals and everyone who shares this vision. We hope that the work of all of our hands, hearts, and minds joined around our globe will one day soon bring about the end of poverty.

Introduction

Opening Our Eyes to How We Can End Poverty in Our Day

The future comes one day at a time.

— Dean Acheson,
American statesman

Can we end poverty in our day if each of us decides to act? Is it really possible? Every morning as we open our eyes, a new day beckons, full of possibility. It is unwritten history—what happens during the course of the day is ours to author. We created this book, and trust that you picked it up, because we not only care about poverty in our world but also believe that this is *our day* to end it. Together we have many new chapters to write.

This book doesn't give extended analyses or mountains of data relating to all the complex issues surrounding poverty. We expect that you already know enough about poverty that you too find it intolerable. What you *will* find here is what *you* can do, starting today, to help end the long night of extreme poverty that more than a billion people in our world now endure.

Some students asked a rabbi how we know when night is over. One asked, "Is it when it is light enough that you can see an animal and tell if it is a goat or a sheep?"

"No," he replied.

"Is it when you look in the distance and can distinguish a fig tree from an olive tree?" suggested another.

"No," the rabbi answered. "We know the night has ended and the day has begun when we can look in the face of a stranger and recognize them as our brother or sister."

If we look in the face of others around the world and recognize them as our brothers and sisters, the night has indeed ended and a new day has begun—our day to end poverty. It is a *good* morning.

Opening Our Eyes

Once we wake up to global poverty, we see all kinds of connections. We see ourselves reflected in others half a world away. We see poverty around the world echoed in the United States. We see how the threads of poverty, health, education, and the environment are tightly interwoven. We see the relationships among how children grow, how women are treated, and how families fare.

Poverty is more than just a lack of money—it is a lack of opportunity, rights, and resources. It is created by ill health and poor or no health care, inadequate housing and transportation, illiteracy, and racial and gender discrimination. It can be affected by things as personal as one's actions and as uncontrollable as the weather. Poverty is caused by things as small as lacking a few dollars of credit and as large as war, national debt, and international trade policies. It is affected by things as immediate as access to clean water and as long range as the state of the environment. Poverty is influenced by things as pervasive as racism and sexism and as isolated as an accident or event in someone's life. As much as we might long for a simple explanation for poverty, or a single solution to end it, we must tackle it as the complex, interrelated challenge that it is.

But here's some good news: Just as the problems are interconnected, so too are the solutions. Solving one part of the problem can have a positive ripple effect. Consider water, for instance. By providing clean, accessible water to a family or village in sub-Saharan Africa, the women and children no longer spend hours lugging water from a distant source and are spared from many waterborne illnesses. As a result, they now have time and good health, so adults can generate income and children can learn. With accessible water, crops can be irrigated, which together with fertilizer and better seeds dramatically increases crop production. With more food, family members are no longer malnourished, are strengthened to stave off or recover from illness, and are better able to earn a living and prepare for the future. That one action of providing clean water is more than just a drop in the bucket; from it flow all sorts of lifesaving, poverty-ending benefits to individuals, families, villages, and ultimately the world.

Our generation is the first to have the resources, technology, and knowledge to end poverty. But it won't be easy. Eradicating poverty calls for a comprehensive approach that ensures every person has the rights, opportunities, and resources to secure an income and the necessary food, health care, education, clean water, housing, and transportation to move or stay out of poverty. Eliminating poverty calls for partnerships large and small to transform our environment, trade policies, and international development. Ending poverty calls for direct actions to ease immediate suffering and systemic change to implement long-term solutions. We will shape the end of poverty by how we use our resources close at hand and how we increase the resources of those far away. All we need is the will to act.

A Millennium Dream

In the year 2000, leaders from around the world gathered at the United Nations' Millennium Summit. They were drawn together by a vision of our world in 2015 in which extreme hunger and poverty are dramatically reduced, all children go to school, girls and women have equal chances, far fewer children die from preventable causes, and more mothers have healthy births and live to see their children grow up. They envisioned fewer people suffering from HIV/AIDS, malaria, and other diseases. They saw many more people with clean water and sanitation, the earth protected to support us all, and nations working in partnership so that all can develop and sustain sufficiency.

This extraordinary vision—comprehensive, inclusive, and ambitious but actually achievable—was captured in a document they called the UN Millennium Declaration. Through it world leaders committed their nations to reaching the eight UN Millennium Development Goals that outline the broad vision and to establishing specific, time-bound, measurable targets to guide and assess our progress toward the goals.

UN Millennium Development Goals

Goal 1
Eradicate extreme hunger and poverty

While pursuing the ultimate goal of eradicating extreme hunger and poverty, the target for 2015 is to reduce by half the proportion of people whose income is less than $1 a day and the proportion of people who suffer from hunger.

Reflect for a moment on the power of the word *eradicate,* which means, literally, to tear out by the roots. The ultimate goal is not just to trim the most obvious manifestations of poverty—which could grow back—but rather to get at the root causes and remove them so that poverty is a thing of the past, gone forever.

Currently, 1 billion people live on less than $1 a day.

Note that when "$1 a day" is used to measure global poverty (the official term is "US$1 a day purchasing power parity"), it does *not* mean, as one might think, that people in other countries are living on what a U.S. dollar, converted into local currency, could buy—which might be a fair amount if local prices are low. It means that people are living on the equivalent of *what a U.S. dollar could buy in the United States.* Think about what a dollar could buy in the United States: say, half a pound of rice and a couple of bananas. That is what those living on $1 a day have to survive on in their own countries.

Goal 2
Achieve universal primary education

Ensure that, by 2015, children everywhere, boys and girls alike, will be able to complete a full course of primary schooling.

Currently, 100 million children of primary school age are not in school.

Goal 3
Promote gender equality and empower women

Eliminate gender disparity in primary education, preferably by 2005, and in all levels of education no later than 2015.

About two-thirds of the world's adult illiterate population are women, and in some regions nearly half of all women are reported to be illiterate, according to the UNESCO Institute for Statistics' latest literacy estimates.

Goal 4
Reduce child mortality

Reduce by two-thirds, between 1990 and 2015, the mortality rate among children under five.

Currently, twenty-eight thousand children die every day from largely preventable malnutrition and disease.

Goal 5
Improve maternal health

Reduce by three-quarters, between 1990 and 2015, the maternal mortality rate.

Currently, five hundred thousand women die in childbirth each year.

Goal 6
Combat HIV/AIDS, malaria, and other diseases

By 2015 have halted and begun to reverse the spread of HIV/AIDS and the incidence of malaria and other major diseases.

At the end of 2006, approximately 39.5 million people worldwide were living with HIV/AIDS, 2.3 million of whom are children; Africa has 12 million AIDS orphans. Currently, at least 1 million deaths occur every year due to malaria.

Goal 7
Ensure environmental sustainability

Integrate the principles of sustainable development into country policies and programs, reverse the loss of environmental resources, and reduce by half, by 2015, the proportion of people without sustainable access to safe drinking water and basic sanitation. Achieve significant improvement in the lives of at least 100 million slum dwellers by 2020.

Currently, 1 billion people do not have access to clean water, and 2 billion don't have improved sanitation.

Goal 8

Develop a global partnership for development

Includes aims to further develop a trading and financial system (with a commitment to good governance, development, and poverty reduction); address the specific needs of the least-developed countries, with debt relief and more-generous official development assistance for countries committed to poverty reduction; address the special needs of landlocked developing countries and small island developing states; and deal comprehensively with the debt problem of developing countries. Targets also include addressing youth work and access to essential drugs and new technologies.

The UN Millennium Project estimates that it will take an additional $75 billion annual developing-country investment to meet the UN Millennium Development Goals by 2015. If U.S. foreign aid increased by 1 percent of the federal budget, we could provide our share to meet the goals.

Despite the fact that African countries have paid back $10 billion more than the amount of loans received between 1970 and 2002, the skyrocketing interest rates of the late 1970s and the early 1980s mean they still owe nearly $300 billion.

An Impossible Dream?

It's a nice dream, but is it really possible? Won't hunger always haunt children in developing countries? Pragmatic world leaders, hardly misty-eyed dreamers, tell us we really can achieve these goals. We've already come a long way. In 1990, forty thousand children died each day from largely preventable malnutrition and disease. Now twelve thousand children's lives are saved every day because of basic health measures provided through the Child Survival Fund and other forms of private and foreign aid from the United States and other countries.

Despite the skeptics who point only to discouraging news coming out of Africa, more than two-thirds of sub-Saharan African countries have held democratic elections since 2000. Many African and other countries are experiencing economic growth. In the decade leading to this new millennium, 130 million people moved out of extreme poverty. We have the knowledge and the resources to continue the progress and help at least half of the 1 billion people living on less than $1 a day move out of extreme poverty. The UN Millennium Development Goals are a dream we can realize, a promise we can keep.

Living the Dream

To make this dream of ending poverty a reality, each of us plays an important role. There is no single solution, no one individual who can achieve it all, no matter how rich or famous. It calls for all of us to contribute in a variety of large and small ways as a fundamental expression of our responsibility as human beings. Apollo astronaut Rusty Schweikert once said, "We aren't passengers on spaceship earth, we're the crew. We aren't residents on this planet, we're citizens. The difference in both cases is responsibility." *Our Day to End Poverty* was created to support each one of us in fulfilling our responsibility as citizens to eliminate poverty on our planet.

Of course there is a role for heads of state and government. There are roles for organizations and corporations. There are many ways religious institutions can contribute and ways for the financial sector to get involved.

And there is a role for each of us as individuals. We created *Our Day to End Poverty* out of the belief that each of us can and must help, starting wherever we are, right now. No one person or group can do everything, but everyone can and must do something. Each of us has gifts, interests, skills, passions, and concerns to bring to the challenge. "I am only one, but still I am one," Helen Keller once said. "I cannot do everything, but still I can do something; I will not refuse to do something I can do."

Whether we take five minutes at a time, five hours a week, or a lifetime, let's do what we can to end poverty in our day. Eleanor Roosevelt affirmed, "The future belongs to those who believe in the beauty of their dreams." Together we *can* transform our dream of a world without poverty into reality.

Looking at the Day Ahead

The Structure of Our Day

We designed this book to connect with your day, from breakfast to bedtime. Whether it's thinking about lunch or reading before bed, you may discover connections between your day and the daily lives of people around the world. Of course, no two people have identical days, and you may find that some of the chapters don't correspond to your actual day at all. Our intention isn't to present a timeline of your exact day, nor do we expect that you will take these actions every hour of your day or at a particular time. Rather, the chapters are meant to suggest how in the course of our days we can both identify with the experiences of others and take action so that, at the end of our day, we will have made a difference.

You'll find here twenty-four chapters divided into three parts: Morning, Afternoon and Evening. In addition to this metaphoric organization, each of the three parts reflects the UN Millennium Development Goals and addresses the issues of hunger, education, work, community and relationships, health care, sustainable environmental practices, and finance.

We have also concluded each part with a chapter that provides more thoughts for shaping your own personal involvement through giving, volunteering, and advocating.

Each chapter offers stories of people like you, who are making a difference. Listen to their voices. Glimpse their visions. Draw inspiration from them as you consider the actions *you* will take.

In each chapter you will also find "Imagine This..." sections—what-if scenarios that invite you to think creatively, expansively, and deeply about poverty and how we can end it. We invite you to reflect on these questions and discuss them with others. Take time to wonder and see where they lead you.

Actions for Our Day

Each of us has much to give, and each of us has different things to offer as we open our eyes, minds, hearts, hands, and very selves to bringing about a new day of "enough" for the world. As you peruse these pages, look for the actions that seem right for you. Each chapter suggests ways to learn more, to contribute, to serve, and to live so that together we can end poverty.

By *learning* about specific topics, we will begin to better understand causes as well as possible solutions to the problems. In each chapter we suggest ways you can *contribute* in addition to writing a check.

We carefully deliberated the use of the word *serve.* We felt that *help* often implies inequality: "you need me, but I don't really need you." *Serving* is at its strongest when it is performed with an attitude of equality and reciprocity and thus recognizes that we need each other. Each of us, regardless of where or how we live, has strengths as well as needs; in relationship we achieve a wholeness no one can achieve alone.

Rounding out the actions is a call to *live* your commitments and your passion. *Live* suggestions might transform your life. How much are you willing to risk? How far do you really want to push the envelope? What are you ready for or excited about? How might changes to the way you and your family live contribute to ending the poverty we see all around us?

We're All in This Together

Remember: as you take action, you don't have to go it alone! Taking action with others can be even more satisfying, sustainable, and downright fun. And it will make an even bigger impact. Think about which actions you would like to take with a friend or family member. Flip through the pages together and see what grabs you. Are there actions that inspire you to engage people in your workplace, religious community, or civic group?

At the end of this book is a short guide to making a difference in your school, your workplace, and your place of worship. Ending poverty is all about building community, and you can start close to home, often acting with those you care about every day.

At the end of each series of action possibilities is good news in a short paragraph called *Actions Make a Difference.* Your actions, too, *will* make a difference!

You have already made a contribution: you have bought this book, and its net author profits are donated to nonprofit organizations dedicated to ending poverty. Whether you take another action or many, even a small effort can contribute to ending poverty in our lifetime. Whatever your bank account or education, age or political perspective, experience or skills, you can make a difference because effecting change isn't a function of any one of these. It's a function of your commitment and your hope, your willingness to take action and just begin. One day at a time.

Anne Frank wrote during the Holocaust in an essay titled "Give," "How lovely to think that no one need wait a moment, we can start now, start slowly changing the world." Let's get started. It is our day to end poverty.

PART I

Morning

CHAPTER 1

Break the Fast

"When you wake up in the morning, Pooh," said Piglet at last, "what's the first thing you say to yourself?"

"What's for breakfast?" said Pooh. "What do you say, Piglet?"

"I say, I wonder what's going to happen exciting today?" said Piglet.

Pooh nodded thoughtfully. "It's the same thing," he said.

— A. A. MILNE, *WINNIE THE POOH*

Wake-up Call

Mornings find most of us stumbling around, starting a pot of coffee, pouring the cereal, or keeping the toast from burning. Some of us are getting the morning news, mentally running through appointments and to-do lists, or just trying to get the kids off to school or ourselves out the door. We're usually too groggy to make the connection between breakfast and something exciting happening that day.

But here's an eye-opener: breakfast literally means "breaking the fast"—ending a period without food. Although most of us feel hopeless when we see images of famine—children with matchstick arms and skeletal parents—it is now possible to break the fast of starvation and ease the most severe hunger in our world. New early-warning systems (of coming drought, for example) are giving the world a heads-up that we can use to avert starvation that is unprecedented. The United Nations now has a Central Emergency Response Fund to respond more quickly and effectively to emergencies.

Together we can "break the fast" of acute hunger and starvation to achieve UN Millennium Development Goal 1: eradicating extreme hunger and poverty, with a target of reducing by half by 2015 the proportion of people who suffer from hunger.

We still need to make sure that there is enough emergency relief money, that food aid is delivered quickly, and that recipient countries are prepared to distribute it effectively. We can focus attention on all of the hunger emergencies, not just the few that capture media and political attention, and we can support long-term solutions to the problems of ongoing hunger so that people are less vulnerable when emergencies of drought and famine strike. That's exciting.

Imagine This...

It would take only pennies. If developed countries gave a penny more per person every three days to the UN Central Emergency Response Fund, we could have enough to meet the urgent need for food to prevent starvation during emergencies, according to Oxfam International.

The United States currently gives $10—the cost of a movie ticket or a couple of rentals—per person each year for humanitarian assistance. Because we are the richest country in the world, we give more than any other, but we give a smaller amount per person than do nine other countries.

Getting Off to a Good Start

LEARN

☐ Read more about hunger in the United States and around the world in Bread for the World's annual report on the state of hunger, which can be downloaded or ordered **<bread.org>**.

Explore the other resources prepared by the Bread for the World Institute.

☐ Visit the UN World Food Programme **<wfp.org>** to learn more about world hunger, what WFP is doing about it, and how you can help.

☐ Get to know such organizations as the Center on Budget and Policy Priorities **<cbpp.org>**, the Food Research and Action Center **<frac.org>**, the Institute for Food and Development Policy **<foodfirst.org>**, Oxfam International **<oxfam.org>**, RESULTS **<results.org>**, and World Vision **<worldvision.org>**—all of which have Web sites, reports, newsletters, and conferences that are excellent information and action resources.

☐ Have some serious fun with children. Download Food Force, a video game developed by the UN World Food Programme to teach children about world hunger **<food-force.com>**. Players work to get food aid to a fictional country in need, overcoming challenges and discovering the thrill of working to solve a serious global problem.

☐ Participate in Oxfam's Fast for a World Harvest to deepen your firsthand understanding of hunger. Involve others by organizing a world hunger banquet to dramatize global food distribution, coordinating a one-meal fast and donating the cost of the skipped meal, or planning a full-day fast and collecting pledges. Visit Oxfam for planning resources.

☐ Watch the one-hour documentary *Silent Killer: The Unfinished Campaign Against Hunger* (2005) with family, friends, neighbors, colleagues, or members of your place of worship and talk about how you can respond **<silentkillerfilm.org>**.

☐ Gather a group from your religious community to study hunger and your faith tradition's response. Use resources prepared by your religious body or other resources such as Hunger No More, Bread for the World's curriculum for churches and synagogues, and materials from MAZON: A Jewish Response to Hunger **<mazon.org>**.

☐ Refer to *community kitchens* instead of the more dated term *soup kitchens,* which conjures up stereotypes of who is hungry and what is served. *Community kitchens* reminds us that we are all part of a community and that this is where some in our community come for a free, nourishing meal and others provide food from their own overflowing pantries and gardens.

☐ Check out the other chapters in this book that discuss various aspects of hunger: chapters 6, 9, 10, and 17.

CONTRIBUTE

☐ Click on **<fighthunger.org>** or **<thehungersite.com>** to help feed a child. It's free, it takes only a few seconds, and you can do it every day. You click, and Web site advertisers contribute.

☐ Help the UN World Food Programme feed more hungry people. Every dollar donated for emergency operations can provide one day of food rations for a family of four (in some countries each dollar feeds even more). For instance, just $99 donated can purchase five thousand cups of rice to feed an entire community or support recovery projects in which food aid is used to pay people to rebuild their communities in the wake of humanitarian tragedies **<wfp.org>**.

Understanding hunger at a gut level can change lives. While in college Alex Counts participated in a one-day fast sponsored by Oxfam International and became committed to ending hunger. He volunteered with the antihunger lobby RESULTS, later becoming its legislative director. A trip to Bangladesh ignited his passion for the potential of microcredit—small loans to help people earn a living so that they can produce or purchase enough food and have the resources to withstand Bangladesh's frequent emergencies. Alex now heads the Grameen Foundation, helping millions of families access microcredit and have enough to eat. And it all started with his own one-day fast.

☐ Donate food to community food pantries to meet the urgent needs of hungry people living in the United States, including 13 million hungry children. Find a local food pantry by entering your ZIP code at America's Second Harvest, the nation's largest network of food banks **<secondharvest.org>**.

☐ Engage school, community, and religious groups in events such as Church World Service's CROP Hunger Walk **<churchworldservice.org/crop>**, Share Our Strength's Great American Bake Sale **<strength.org>**, and The Souper Bowl of Caring's Souper Bowl Sunday **<souperbowl.org>** to raise money or collect food for programs serving people who are hungry.

☐ Spur donations of good, leftover food. Encourage restaurants, hotels, caterers, and even universities to donate usable food instead of throwing it away. Done right, it does not violate health code guidelines. For more information about the Bill Emerson Good Samaritan Food Donation Act of 1996, which protects donors from liability, go to the America's Second Harvest Web site **<secondharvest.org>**.

SERVE

- ☐ Prepare and serve meals in a community kitchen for some of our nation's 35 million hungry people.

- ☐ Lend a hand. Volunteer at a local food bank or other program that serves people who are hungry. Visit **<secondharvest.org>** to find a local food bank or food rescue organization that can use your help.

- ☐ Start or help strengthen a food pantry, community kitchen, or other emergency feeding program, with help from World Hunger Year's resource *Serving Up Justice: How to Design an Emergency Feeding Program and Build Community Food Security* **<worldhungeryear.org>**.

- ☐ Write letters to your newspaper and your members of Congress to focus their attention on hunger crises and urge immediate responses to provide humanitarian assistance to ward off starvation and promote long-term solutions. The organizations listed in the "Learn" section provide information and sample letters.

- ☐ Encourage teachers to present lessons on hunger. Check out the resources from Feeding Minds, Fighting Hunger **<feedingminds.org>** and a high school curriculum from kNOw HUNGER **<knowhunger.org>**.

- ☐ Organize World Food Day **<fao.org>** activities in your community to help people learn more about causes of and solutions to world hunger.

LIVE

- ☐ Serve at least one meatless dinner a week, using nonanimal sources of protein that require fewer of the world's resources to produce, or commit to another lifestyle change regarding all the foods you eat: avoid overpackaged foods, or become a "locavore," buying your food from local sources.

- ☐ Assess how much food is wasted in your household and find a way to reduce it.

Actions Make a Difference

Norman Borlaug, awarded the Nobel Peace Prize in 1970 for his efforts to end world hunger and increase international prosperity, is credited with saving 1 billion people from starvation. As director of the Rockefeller Foundation in Mexico and head of an international team of scientists, he created a "green revolution" that developed improved wheat seed, higher-yield rice, and more-efficient use of fertilizer and water to produce larger food crops in Mexico, Pakistan, India, and elsewhere. While a professor at Texas A&M University, Borlaug founded the World Food Prize in 1986 to recognize others who are helping increase the world's food supply and end hunger.

CHAPTER 2

Educate Every Child

Small children are the most powerful learning engines in the known universe.

— DANIEL QUINN, *MY ISHMAEL*

Promises to Keep

January 1 marks the New Year on our calendars, but doesn't September feel like the real start of the year? Maybe it's because we remember our own first day of school, stomach filled with butterflies instead of the breakfast we were too nervous to eat. Or perhaps it's a more recent experience of seeing children head off for their first day of school, backpacks full of newly sharpened pencils and blank notebooks. Going off to school fills a child with promise and unlimited possibility.

It's hard to believe that children in the United States didn't always go to school. Children of slaves were forbidden to learn to read, and farm children were needed for work. (Our school calendar still reflects this history of keeping children out of school when they were needed to harvest crops.) Children once worked in sweatshops to help support the family, and disabled children weren't guaranteed a public education until 1975. Today all children in the United States are guaranteed a public education, although we still have much work to do to make it the best education possible for every student.

Education prepares us for productive futures. UN Millennium Development Goal 2 calls on us to ensure that, by 2015, children everywhere, boys and girls alike, can complete primary school.

Around the world, 100 million children are still waiting for the promise of an education, denied the opportunity because they are girls, because they are needed for work, or because their families living on $1 a day can't afford school fees that average $50 per child in developing countries.

One day education may be so universal that children everywhere will be amazed to read in their history textbooks about a time when children did not go to school. But that time is not yet. Let's make a resolution to act so every child is educated. That's a promise worth keeping.

Imagine This...

Think about the ways your daily life depends on skills you learned in primary school. How did *you* learn to read, write, and do math? Now think about the productivity and the contributions to the world that would be unleashed if *all* of our world's children were able to go to school. Imagine their innovative thinking. Imagine their creative power!

Learning to Change the World

LEARN

☐ Discover the hopeful stories of children who are finally able to attend school. Visit the Web site of the United Nations Girls' Education Initiative **<ungei.org>** and click on "Multimedia," "The Gap Project," and "Real Lives" for stories, photo essays, and videos. E-mail the ones that inspire you most to friends and family.

☐ Interview a teacher, the parent of a school-aged child, or the local Parent Teacher Association president to discover needs and opportunities to strengthen schools. Ask students what they think is needed, too.

☐ Visit the Global Campaign for Education **<campaignfor education.org>** to learn how you can get involved to help meet Millennium Development Goal 2 of all children in primary school by 2015.

☐ Read books, articles, and reports exploring challenges and opportunities in U.S. schools. Good places to start include *Savage Inequalities* by Jonathan Kozol, *Uncertain Lives: Children of Promise, Teachers of Hope* by Robert V. Bullough Jr., *The Silent Epidemic: Perspectives of High School Dropouts* at **<civicenterprises.net>**, and resources from the Education Trust **<edtrust.org>**. Invite others to join you for a book group to read, discuss, and act on these resources.

☐ Learn about what local businesses are doing to provide internships for high school students, then spread the word and support those businesses. Check out Big Picture **<bigpicture.org>** for help.

CONTRIBUTE

☐ Commit to ensuring a girl's education all the way through primary school. For $2,500 a Room to Grow **<roomtogrow.org>** Girls' Scholarship will secure a girl's school participation for ten years.

☐ Visit Web sites such as DonorsChoose **<donorschoose.org>** that post and match teachers' requests with contributions that pay for needed supplies and other expenses large and small.

☐ Round up used but not outdated computers to donate to schools or community programs where children without computers at home can do their homework. Or get involved with such organizations as Computers for Schools

<pcsforschools.org> to get good computers to schools around the world. See chapter 10 for more ideas.

☐ Organize a school-supply drive or a book drive through your school, workplace, civic group, or place of worship. Donate the supplies to a school in the United States or overseas.

☐ Honor a student's graduation with a gift in his or her name to benefit other children's education, such as providing the $50 school fees for a child in a developing country. Learn more from UNICEF **<unicef.org/whatwedo>**.

SERVE

☐ Become a tutor. Go online to review the reading scores of local public schools. Call the school with the lowest scores and volunteer to help. Or volunteer with a community tutoring or Head Start program.

☐ Organize a team to fix up a local school (painting, planting, donating books and computers, providing comfortable furnishings—any need that can be filled). Ask teachers and principals what kind of support they need most.

☐ Involve others to plan your community's participation in the Global Campaign for Education's Global Action Week to focus attention on global education. Planning resources are available at **<campaignforeducation.org/resources>** and at **<ei-ie.org/globalactionweek>**.

☐ Join with others who are advocating legislation that seeks to eliminate school fees in the developing world. RESULTS **<results.org>**, a grassroots lobby dedicated to ending world hunger and poverty, is taking action on this initiative.

Sister Schools began in 1988 when Terry McGill was traveling in Uganda and saw incredible poverty. He asked himself, *If I really am the kind of person I like to think I am, what should I do about this?* After returning home to Seattle, McGill was invited by local teachers to share the images of Ugandan school life with their students. Children at every school asked if they could send things to Uganda. Expecting to receive a few items he could fit into an extra suitcase, McGill agreed. To his surprise each school contributed hundreds of pounds of clothing and school supplies. Since then McGill has spoken in more than seventy-five schools to thousands of students and teachers, who have sent more than 150,000 pounds of supplies to their counterparts in Uganda. McGill has seen the life-changing impact of neighbor-to-neighbor sharing, even if one neighbor is half a world away.

☐ Start Sister Schools. Establish a relationship between a school in a developing country and your school, workplace, civic group, place of worship, or other group **<sisterschools.org>**. (Read Terry McGill's story above.)

☐ Travel to teach. If you have training as an educator, contact a service or development organization to explore a short- or long-term volunteer stint as a teacher or a teacher trainer. Look for options through **<volunteerinternational.org>** or use an online search engine to find numerous opportunities that match your talents and resources.

☐ Plan a work program to help build a school in a developing country. Assemble a team through your school, workplace, civic group, place of worship, or community. Again, search the Internet for current opportunities.

Children can be our teachers. The Uganda Rural Development and Training Programme Girls School in Kagadi uses a "two-generation" approach to education. Every semester the girls lead a parent workshop during which families plan "back home projects" to raise the standard of living in their household. Projects include creating or expanding a garden; building a latrine, kitchen, or house; and starting an income-generating venture. The girls become the agents of change in their families and inspire their parents to get involved in further educational ventures such as adult literacy programs. *Source:* **<urdt.net>**

- ☐ Assist in helping low-income students find college-funding sources. There may be sources in your own community, or you can find them through research in libraries or on the Internet. One such example is the Horatio Alger Association **<horatioalger.org/scholarships>**.

LIVE

- ☐ Read to a child in your life every day. Talk about what has happened in the story and what might happen.
- ☐ Run for your local school board.
- ☐ Make a commitment to one first-grader and her family that you will support her educational success from now through her completion of college.
- ☐ Honor your own desires for continuing education.
- ☐ Commit to a TV-free day at least once a week, with a more ambitious television-free goal in mind. Instead read for pleasure, engage in conversation, play games, and spend time outside.

Actions Make a Difference

Today three out of every four girls in developing countries attend primary school. This is a vast improvement over what it was just a decade or two ago. When girls are educated, economic productivity improves, mother and infant death rates decline, families have fewer children, environmental management increases, and the health, well-being, and educational prospects for the next generation improve significantly. And get this: providing girls with *one extra year* of education beyond the average boosts their eventual wages by 10 to 20 percent.

CHAPTER 3

Make Work Pay

Your profession is not what brings home your paycheck. Your profession is what you were put on earth to do. With such passion and such intensity that it becomes spiritual in calling.

— VINCENT VAN GOGH, DUTCH POSTIMPRESSIONIST PAINTER

Another Day, Another Dollar

How do you feel about the work you do? Most of us at some time have had one of those jobs where the minutes drag by and we count the days until we can finally pick up a paycheck and enjoy the weekend. Then there are those jobs that feel more like a calling, where the time flies and at the end of the day we have a deep sense of satisfaction and accomplishment. And at some time in our lives, each of us has most likely known what it feels like to be unemployed or underemployed.

"Working poor" should be an oxymoron, yet the reality is that millions of people in our nation and billions around the world work hard at jobs every day and still find themselves in poverty. In the United States, about 37 million people (one in eight) live in poverty even though most of them work. Around the world one out of every five people earns less than $1 a day. At worst millions are forced to beg and scavenge or are trafficked as modern-day

With living wages and full employment, we can create a path out of poverty. UN Millennium Development Goal 1, eradicating extreme hunger and poverty, has a target of cutting in half by 2015 the proportion of people whose income is less than $1 a day.

slaves—bought and sold into prostitution, domestic servitude, or agricultural work.

Let's work for a world where everyone's work pays, and people have the job training, health coverage, child care, and other services they need in order to do their work. Let's work to establish a reliable safety net for when people's jobs fall through or when they just don't pay a living wage.

Imagine This…

Imagine working full-time, year-round in a minimum-wage job and *still* being poor. In recent decades the minimum wage has been less than what is necessary to even reach the poverty line, as established by the U.S. Department of Health and Human Services. Based on the 2006 poverty line of $16,600 for a family of three, the federal minimum wage would need to be set at almost $8 per hour for the family to break through the poverty line. What does it feel like to work hard, play by the rules, and still be poor?

Working to End Poverty

LEARN

☐ Visit the Let Justice Roll Living Wage Campaign Web site **<letjusticeroll.org>** for information, resources, and action ideas for your place of worship or community group.

☐ Get new insights into work and poverty challenges in the United States by reading *Nickel and Dimed: On (Not) Getting By in America* by Barbara Ehrenreich; *No Shame in My Game: The Working Poor in the Inner City* by Katherine S. Newman; *Raise the Floor: Wages and Policies That Work for All of Us* by Holly Sklar, Laryssa Mykyta, and Susan Wefald; and *Growing*

Up Poor: A Literary Anthology edited by Robert Coles and Randy Testa with Michael Coles. Read them on your own or suggest them for your book group or a class in your place of worship.

- ☐ Order a documentary DVD or book from **<freetheslaves.net>** and view or read it with others to learn about modern-day slavery and how we can help end it. Download the free Education Pack to use in schools or with a religious youth group.

- ☐ Explore Wider Opportunities for Women **<wowonline.org>** for strategies for improving women's employment, including the Family Economic Self-Sufficiency Project, Work4Women, and Workplace Solutions.

- ☐ Invite a speaker who is knowledgeable about human trafficking to speak at your workplace, civic group, or place of worship to raise awareness and develop advocates. Possible sources of speakers include refugee and immigration groups.

- ☐ Read chapter 11 about microcredit—small loans for self-employment—to learn more about how this tool helps people profit from their hard work and move out of poverty. See chapter 6 for ways to support agricultural workers.

- ☐ Watch, and discuss with friends, movies about who manufactures what and how, such as *Mardi Gras: Made in China* (2005), about Mardi Gras beads (used as a fund-raiser for Hurricane Katrina recovery efforts), and *Waging a Living* (2006), a PBS documentary that tests the mantra "get a job" to see if the "working poor" can pull themselves and their families out of poverty, tracking the ups and downs of four ethnically diverse Americans living below the poverty line as they struggle to make ends meet over a three-year period.

☐ Refer to chapter 7 for resources to ensure that the goods you purchase were produced without labor exploitation.

CONTRIBUTE

☐ Donate good-quality work suits to organizations supporting entry into the workforce, such as Dress for Success **<dressforsuccess.org>**, so that unemployed people can make a good impression in job interviews. Encourage friends and colleagues to do the same, or coordinate a Send One Suit Week drive.

☐ Contact a high-quality child-care program and then work with others to raise funds for child-care scholarships or subsidies for low-income families. Or house a weekday child-care program in your place of worship. Having available, affordable, high-quality child care can make or break someone's ability to get and keep a job.

☐ Shop at stores like Ten Thousand Villages **<tenthousandvillages.com>** that provide a market for people in developing countries to sell and profit from their work.

☐ Contribute to organizations working to protect people from exploitation and provide sustainable livings, such as Shared Hope International **<sharedhope.org>** and Women for Women International **<womenforwomen.org>**.

Don't underestimate your expertise. A few years ago, the Foleys, a Maine couple who own a bed-and-breakfast (B&B), traveled to Armenia to consult with Armenian B&B owners to help develop the hospitality industry there. As International Executive Service Corps **<iesc.org>** volunteers, they drew on their experience to offer suggestions about services, pricing, and marketing.

SERVE

☐ Sign up to help with free tax preparation so low-income workers receive all of the benefits for which they are eligible, including the Earned Income Tax Credit, or work with your place of worship to host such a site. For more information visit the Center on Budget and Policy Priorities Web site **<cbpp.org>**. For a list of VITA (Volunteer Income Tax Assistance) sites, visit **<irs.gov>** or call 1-800-TAX-1040.

☐ Partner with a family transitioning off TANF (Temporary Assistance for Needy Families, commonly known as welfare) to provide emotional support and practical assistance. Work through a welfare-to-work site or a community social service agency to arrange the partnership.

☐ Help prepare résumés or polish job interview skills. Work through a community agency to connect with people who need such assistance.

☐ Volunteer to visit schools in low-income communities to talk about your job. Encourage others to participate in "career days."

☐ Advocate for programs and policies that support people's ability to work and provide for their families, such as the minimum wage, the Earned Income Tax Credit, child-care subsidies, unemployment insurance, and safety-net programs that protect children from the worst aspects of poverty. These programs include food stamps; the Special Supplemental Nutrition Program for Women, Infants, and Children (WIC); Medicaid; the State Children's Health Insurance Program; and Temporary Assistance for Needy Families. Organizations such as the Center on Budget and Policy Priorities **<cbpp.org>**

and the Children's Defense Fund **<childrensdefense.org>** provide resources to support advocates.

- ☐ Participate in grassroots organizing for change in your community. ACORN, the Association of Community Organizations for Reform Now **<acorn.org>**, is the nation's largest community organization of low- and moderate-income families in neighborhood chapters in cities in the United States and other countries, working to improve job conditions, wages, housing, health care, schools, neighborhood safety, and more.

- ☐ Be a voice in your community for more local job training and education funding.

- ☐ Through your workplace arrange for internships, apprenticeships, and "job shadowing" opportunities for young people who might not otherwise have ready access to work culture, opportunities, and connections that will prepare them for success when they enter the workforce as adults.

- ☐ Speak out against human trafficking. Connect with an organization like Free the Slaves **<freetheslaves.net>** for advocacy information and support. Call the Trafficking Information and Referral Hotline at 1-888-373-7888 for a referral to an appropriate organization that can help if you think someone is a victim of human trafficking. If the suspected victim is a minor, contact local child protection authorities.

- ☐ Volunteer with a community organization to help eligible families receive antipoverty assistance such as food stamps, Medicaid or the State Children's Health Insurance Program, and child support.

LIVE

- ☐ Pay a living wage if you employ people in your business—and encourage others to do so.
- ☐ Pay a living wage if you employ people in your home (for instance, to provide child care or house cleaning).
- ☐ Provide employees with more job training and/or help with child care, if you employ people.
- ☐ Live on less. Reduce your monthly living expenses by a certain percentage and commit the money saved to an organization helping people move out of poverty.

Actions Make a Difference

Mildred Lacen works full-time while raising her three children and three foster children in New York. When her taxes were prepared at a free tax assistance site and she qualified for the Earned Income Tax Credit, she received a $7,000 refund—more than a quarter of what she earned working the previous year. It not only helped her pay bills but, she reports proudly, "I was able to put that away and save it toward a down payment on my house." If every qualifying family with children in our nation received all of the cash benefits, like the Earned Income Tax Credit, and food assistance for which they are eligible, according to the Children's Defense Fund, child poverty would be reduced by 20 percent and the number of families living in extreme poverty would be reduced by 70 percent.

CHAPTER 4

Care for Our Children

It is easier to build strong children than to repair broken men.

— Frederick Douglass, American journalist and abolitionist

At Least One Adult

Every one of us begins life as a baby who needs the care of an adult. For most babies, cries are heard, needs are met, and trust is affirmed. But for many, cries go unanswered, tears are unnoticed, trust is betrayed, and basic needs remain unfulfilled. Whether from love fulfilled or hopes disappointed, as adults we know at the deepest level how important it is for children to be loved and protected, to have at least one adult who cares for them and provides what they need.

Around the world right now, children are at play. In Boston a father pushes his toddler in a swing while a five-year-old climbs on a jungle gym under the watchful eye of her grandmother. Teenagers play pickup basketball with a counselor in a Bronx Boys and Girls Club. Indonesian boys trade pet crabs while their mothers cook nearby. California boys swap baseball cards during recess until the teacher calls them in.

All children should be nurtured and protected. Meeting the UN Millennium Development Goals will help give children the basic resources they need and deserve.

Around the world right now, children are also at risk. A four-year-old girl in Iowa waits for adoption, just one of five hundred thousand U.S. children in foster care. A twelve-year-old boy in sub-Saharan Africa works long hours every day, as do 218 million other children around the world. An eleven-year-old in Thailand waits on a corner—one of 2 million children exploited through prostitution and pornography worldwide. In New York a teen's parents are incarcerated, so she is being raised by her grandparent as are 2.5 million other children in the United States. A toddler in Botswana lost his mother to AIDS as have an estimated 13 million other orphans. Children are at risk everywhere; many are with adults who deeply, desperately want to care for them but are unable to without various forms of support.

Building Strong Children

To build strong children, we must lay a foundation of sufficient household income and nutrition, put up a strong framework of education and health care, and overlay a sturdy roof of protection from the storms of violence, displacement, and natural disasters. Most important, to build strong children, all require at least one caring adult with the support and the resources to nurture and protect them.

> ***"People often innocently ask, 'Why did you adopt? Why not just have more of your "own" children?' And I used to become mildly offended by those questions. But now I just chuckle as I think about who my 'own' children are. They are my foster son, my stepson, my two birth daughters, and my adopted daughter and son. They are all my 'own' children, even though each came to be my child in very different ways. And I often wonder what a different place the world might be if we no longer applied the labels of 'adopted' or 'foster' or 'step' and just cared for each child in our lives as our 'own,' regardless of the circumstances that brought them to us."***
>
> — Jeff Keenan, co-author, *Our Day to End Poverty*

Imagine This...

Imagine the difference it would make if 9 million of us decided to sponsor a child, for about $35 per month, through an organization such as Save the Children or World Vision. Who would benefit? The sponsored children would benefit, to be sure, but so would their families and their entire communities, as sponsor funds are typically used for education, health care, clean water, and other projects that have broad benefits. Most of all we ourselves would gain an ongoing relationship with a child living in another community. As a result of our action, many lives would be transformed, not the least of which would be our own.

Showing We Care

LEARN

- ☐ Spend time with children in a homeless shelter, a Head Start program, or other setting and listen to their hopes and fears, dreams and disappointments.

- ☐ Explore the Children's Defense Fund's Web site **<childrensdefense.org>** to learn more about the needs of America's children and how you can help. Read its annual publication, *The State of America's Children.*

- ☐ Learn more about the needs of the world's children and what we can do. Check out the resources of Save the Children **<savethechildren.org>** and UNICEF **<unicef.org>**, including UNICEF's annual report, *The State of the World's Children.*

- ☐ Glimpse the world through a child's eyes and words as recorded by Jonathan Kozol in *Amazing Grace: The Lives of Children and the Conscience of a Nation*; Alex Kotlowitz in

There Are No Children Here: The Story of Two Boys Growing Up in the Other America; and Robert Coles in *The Spiritual Life of Children.* Or read books like *Terrify No More: Young Girls Held Captive and the Daring Undercover Operation to Win Their Freedom* by Gary A. Haugen and Gregg Hunter to understand how people like you have helped rescue children who are trafficked. Invite others to read and discuss these books with you.

☐ Inform yourself about goods you intend to purchase to ensure that they were not produced using child labor. Look for the RugMark label, Fair Trade Certified goods, and other labels and trademarks of goods produced without child labor. See chapter 7 for more ideas.

☐ Read chapters 2, 3, 5, and 21 on education, paid work, child health, and maternal and newborn health—all of which have a significant impact on the well-being of children.

CONTRIBUTE

☐ Donate items such as suitcases, backpacks, and sports equipment through the National Foster Parent Association **<nfpainc.org>** or any organization meeting the needs of children.

☐ Give to organizations, many listed in this chapter, that are working to improve the lives of children in the United States and around the world.

☐ Involve children in contributing part of their allowance to a child-serving program; donating their gently used toys, books, and clothes; purchasing requested holiday gifts for low-income children; or raising money for a farm animal through Heifer Project International **<heifer.org>**.

☐ Protect street children around the world from police brutality, trafficking, and other violations of their rights and childhood by giving to organizations like the International Justice Mission **<ijm.org>**, Shared Hope International **<sharedhope.org>**, and Street Kids International **<streetkids.org>**.

SERVE

☐ Engage your place of worship in the annual interfaith National Observance of Children's Sabbaths in October to learn more about the needs of children, explore religious teachings and texts that call on people of faith to care for children, and engage in practical responses to meet their needs and advocate on their behalf. The Children's Defense Fund prepares resources to help you participate.

☐ Support World Vision's Child Sex Tourism Prevention Project, which provides deterrent messages, law enforcement assistance, and prevention programs to protect children **<worldvision.org>**.

☐ Help give a break to grandparent caregivers, foster parents, and single parents so they can recharge their batteries. Start a support group or drop-off child-care program one afternoon or evening a month in your place of worship, community center, or school.

☐ Volunteer with a child abuse or runaway hotline or a "warm line" that provides support to struggling parents before a situation turns into a crisis.

- ☐ Become a Court Appointed Special Advocate **<nationalcasa.org>**, a trained volunteer appointed by judges to represent the best interests of abused and neglected children.

- ☐ Advocate for programs and policies that protect children in the United States from poverty, hunger, homelessness, violence, and other problems. Call for health care, child care, and other important supports and safety nets to help families nurture, protect, and provide for their children. The Children's Defense Fund offers information, resources, and support **<childrensdefense.org>**.

- ☐ Speak up for the needs of children around the world. Connect with the advocacy resources and support offered by many of the organizations listed in this chapter.

- ☐ Travel to a developing country (alone or with like-minded friends) and arrange to spend time with children and families to learn firsthand what needs to be done. Ask what resources you can bring that would be helpful, such as books, diapers, and health-care supplies.

- ☐ Apply for an internship overseas with the International Justice Mission **<ijm.org>** to personally help those who suffer abuse and oppression every day.

Formerly trafficked children are finding safe havens thanks to the work of dedicated organizations and individuals around the world. The International Justice Mission (IJM) has partnered with aftercare facilities like the one in South Asia that provides love, safety, and schooling to young girls like Manna. IJM rescued Manna from a soundproof dungeon in which she was raped every day for the profit of her captors. Because IJM helped build a case to put her captors behind bars, Manna now studies to be a social worker in the aftercare facility that cares for her. *Source:* **<ijm.org>**

LIVE

- ☐ Tell the children in your life that you love them and will always do whatever you can to be there for them.

- ☐ Sponsor a child. Sponsorship organizations include Children International **<children.org>**, Compassion International **<compassion.com>**, Plan **<plan-international.org>**, and others in this chapter. Be sure to use the tips from the Better Business Bureau's Wise Giving Alliance **<give.org>** for selecting a child sponsorship agency.

- ☐ Mentor a child in need of a caring, supportive adult in his or her life. Become a Big Brother or Big Sister **<bbbsa.org>** or forge a relationship with a teenager who is growing up in foster care without being adopted and who faces young adulthood without a guiding parent figure.

- ☐ Become a foster or adoptive parent. The National Foster Parent Association **<nfpainc.org>** and the North American Council on Adoptable Children **<nacac.org>** are just two groups ready to supply you with information about fostering or adopting children in the United States. For international adoption the U.S. Department of State **<travel.state.gov/family>** provides information about adoption laws in particular countries and their official adoption agencies or bureaus.

- ☐ Involve the children in your life in contributing and serving to improve the lives of other children. Children are very inventive and will think of projects and group activities that are just right for them. You can also introduce them to ways they can fight global poverty all their lives by visiting NetAid together **<netaid.org/global_poverty/global-poverty>**.

Actions Make a Difference

According to the UN's International Labour Organization, the number of child workers in Latin America and the Caribbean dropped by about 66 percent between 2000 and 2004; only 5 percent of children in those countries now work, reports the International Programme on the Elimination of Child Labour **<ilo.org>**, which helped several countries enact measures to eliminate the worst forms of child labor.

CHAPTER 5

Give All Children Healthy Futures

Children are one-third of our population and all of our future.

— Select Panel for the Promotion of Child Health, 1981

Growing Commitment to Child Health

Do you remember going kicking and screaming to the doctor's office when you were a child? One six-year-old's screams routinely echo through the pediatrician's office whenever the needle nears her arm. On a recent car ride to the clinic for a booster shot, she was accompanied by her three-year-old brother, who looked into her fear-stricken face and solemnly observed, "Uh-oh. Shots time."

Half a world away in Cambodia, another six-year-old shrinks back in fear as the needle nears her arm to inject a measles vaccine. Despite her cries, the moment represents a joyous triumph against the odds. Such a simple shot puts her on the path to a healthy future—one that is still out of reach for millions of children in developing countries and for 9 million children without health coverage in the United States.

Good health strengthens children, families, and our future. UN Millennium Development Goal 4 challenges us to reduce child deaths, aiming to cut the death rate of children under five by two-thirds by 2015.

We don't need to feel hopeless when we learn that twenty-eight thousand children die of preventable causes each day because we can help reduce these needless deaths right now. There are many simple and inexpensive solutions that could save the lives of 10 million children under five who die each year of largely preventable causes. Antibiotics costing just a few dollars can cure respiratory infections, and oral rehydration salts (sort of like powdered sports drinks) costing just a few pennies can save the lives of children with diarrhea. Deadly, mosquito-borne malaria can be treated with two rounds of drugs and prevented with bed nets that cost only about $5 each. For just $17 a child can be fully immunized against measles and other killer diseases.

Most doctor visits include measuring height and weight to assure that growth is on target. Let's stand tall and weigh in with our actions and our advocacy so that we measure up as individuals, as nations, and as a world in giving all of our children the health care they deserve.

Imagine This...

The late Jim Grant, who headed up UNICEF, used to keep a packet of oral rehydration salts in his jacket pocket. When talking with others about this powerful solution, he would pull it out so they could see the inexpensive remedy first-hand and realize that it is literally within our reach to save thousands of children's lives around the world. What can you wear or carry with you every day to remind yourself and others that reaching UN Millennium Development Goal 4 of reducing child deaths is within our grasp if we act now?

Taking Our Best Shot at Improving Global Health

LEARN

☐ Discover how you can help spread the word about the availability of free and low-cost health insurance for children in the United States and engage your school, workplace, civic group, or place of worship in this effort. Most of our nation's 9 million uninsured children are eligible for Medicaid or the State Children's Health Insurance Program, but their parents don't know about the program, don't know they are eligible, or aren't sure how to apply. Visit **<coveringkids.org>** to learn more.

☐ Check out the Global Health Council **<globalhealth.org>** and its resources for learning more, advocating, donating, and volunteering. Its list of member organizations provides links to dozens of groups working on global health.

☐ Read Tracy Kidder's book, *Mountains Beyond Mountains,* about the work of Dr. Paul Farmer in Haiti and around the world, to learn more about how we can improve health in developing countries. Its bibliography lists publications for further reading.

CONTRIBUTE

☐ Donate toys, books, and other items to clinics serving children who are poor. The clinics can use the items to entertain children during lengthy waits or even give them to the children to keep.

☐ Support a health program. Visit **<globalgiving.com>** or search *health programs* on the Internet to see options for supporting such programs around the world. You'll find a very large number, so add your geographic location or specific focus to narrow your search. See chapter 8 for tips on selecting reputable organizations for contributions.

☐ If you are a health-care professional, donate a certain number of visits per month to uninsured children. Work with the local school district for referrals.

☐ Raise funds to establish a health clinic in an underserved area. Organize a 5-kilometer Walk for Health, with participants collecting pledges. Launch a Co-pay for Global Health Care campaign and invite co-workers, neighbors, members of your place of worship, and others to donate the equivalent of their health insurance co-pay to an organization providing health care for uninsured children.

☐ Buy toothbrushes and children's toothpaste to donate to programs or schools with high numbers of children living in poverty. Keep in mind that regular dental care is what children need even more than toothbrushes, and work toward that end.

A teenager in suburban Philadelphia belongs to St. Paul's Episcopal Church, which is raising money to buy treated bed nets to prevent deadly malaria in Koraro, Ethiopia. He was astounded to learn that just $5 for one bed net could save a child's life, and he wanted to tell others. He and his pastor presented a program, "Children Saving Children," at an elementary school assembly. He trained members of his high school's National Honor Society to talk with older students about malaria and staffed a table during lunch to educate others and to raise money for the children of Koraro. This effort helped St. Paul's raise more than $5,000 to buy bed nets that could save a thousand young lives.

SERVE

- ☐ Contact your state department of health or community service agency to see if it has a volunteer home-visitor program. Home visitors may provide support and encouragement to new mothers returning home from the hospital and others.

- ☐ Prepare "comfort dolls"—small knitted dolls that are used to protect medical supplies during transport overseas. These protective wraps are then stuffed and distributed as toys to poor children. Visit **<icross.ca/project.htm>** for knitting patterns and other information to participate in this project.

- ☐ Advocate for policy improvements for children's health. To speak out on global children's health, visit **<globalhealth.org>** and click on "Take Action" for advocacy resources or sign up to receive advocacy information from the Global Health Council. To join others in speaking out for universal child health coverage in the United States, contact the Children's Defense Fund **<childrensdefense.org>**.

- ☐ Sign the online petition of the Campaign for Children's Health Care **<childrenshealthcampaign.org>**. If you have first-hand experience of needing health insurance, share your story with the campaign.

- ☐ Work with your school system, parent/teacher organizations, and others to increase the nutritional value of school meals and to ensure that healthy snacks, not junk food and sugary drinks, are sold on school campuses. Learn more about the communities already working to serve locally (and carefully) grown food in their children's cafeterias. Also help ensure that physical activity is incorporated into the school day so that all children are encouraged to establish healthy exercise habits.

LIVE

- ☐ Model and promote preventive health and wellness, including healthy eating, regular exercise, and not smoking, which can reverse the effects of asthma, obesity, and other public health crises.

- ☐ If you are a health-care professional, offer to care for children who are not citizens and may not qualify for Medicaid or the State Children's Health Insurance Program.

Actions Make a Difference

Even just watching a movie can make a difference. A 1990 documentary for the World Summit for Children titled *341* told of the number of children who would die during the twelve minutes it took to watch the film. World leaders watched the documentary as a child's life slipped away every three seconds—forty thousand per day. Citizen activists met with their senators and representatives and showed them the video. This citizen advocacy prompted Congress to create the Child Survival Fund to provide basic health measures in developing countries. As a result, the lives of twelve thousand children are saved each and every day.

CHAPTER 6

Help Produce a Better Harvest

To say yes, you have to sweat and roll up your sleeves and plunge both hands into life up to the elbows.

— Jean Anouilh, French playwright

Produce a Great Future

Whether it is a child, elbow deep in mud, sloshing water from a hose in the yard, an office worker watering a plant at her desk, a gardener plucking a ripe tomato still warm from the sun, or a farmer harvesting a crop, there is something deeply satisfying about rolling up our sleeves and tending growing plants. That satisfaction is tempered, however, by the inevitable disappointments: seeds that don't sprout, plants riddled with pests, blossoms that fall off the vine, and rain that never comes. "A garden," wrote poet May Sarton, "is always a series of losses set against a few triumphs, like life itself."

> ***We all need sustainable food sources. UN Millennium Development Goal 7 calls for environmental sustainability, and Goal 1 aims to eradicate extreme hunger and poverty.***

No one understands the setbacks of planting and life more than those who farm for their livelihoods. Of the world's 850 million hungry people, half are small-scale farming families (including those who work others' land), dependent on agriculture with all of its challenges.

But by working together, we *can* create triumphs. Irrigation, fertilizer, and better seeds can double or triple crop yields for many struggling farmers. Better training, tools, storage, credit, transportation, and access to markets are also basic, doable solutions. Policies and enforcement to ensure decent living and working conditions help migrant workers and all who farm others' land to thrive, and land rights ensure that people benefit from their own labor.

Let's dig in and support the work of farmers around the world to yield a flourishing future.

Imagine This...

Imagine how small seeds of change can grow into a life-changing difference for families, villages, and children orphaned by AIDS. Through Africa Bridge's microcredit program, for instance, agricultural co-ops offer $500 loans to enable the poorest people to cultivate their own land and grow a cash crop—in southwest Tanzania's case, that's potatoes. Farmers can grow two crops of potatoes every year, with corn and beans planted between the rows.

Africa Bridge **<africabridge.org>** provides four months of education on marketing, ways to grow crops without eroding the soil, and other vital skills. As the co-op grows, more farmers are helped and one person is chosen from each village to go to agricultural school with tuition paid by profits from the co-op. Over three years the co-op can fund another four families.

According to Barry Childs, founder of Africa Bridge, there is an innovative twist: to be in the Africa Bridge co-op, you must adopt a child orphaned by AIDS. A portion of the co-op monies goes to ongoing child care for families with several adopted children. Co-op members are lifting themselves out of poverty with their pride intact: without taking charity, they are also giving hope and homes to AIDS orphans as they put down new roots.

Digging In

LEARN

- ☐ Get inspired by Millennium Villages, which are demonstrating the profound, transformative impact of a comprehensive and integrated approach that includes agricultural advances as well as improved health care, access to water, and other essentials for ending poverty. Read about them at the UN Millennium Project **<unmillenniumproject.org>** and the Millennium Promise **<millenniumpromise.org>**.

- ☐ Visit the Farmworker Health Services Web site **<farmworker health.org>** to learn more about U.S. farmworkers and efforts to improve their access to health care and other services.

- ☐ Read *The End of Poverty: Economic Possibilities for Our Time* by Jeffery Sachs, director of the Millennium Project, on your own, with a book group, or as the basis of a class in your place of worship. Additional resources are available at the Earth Institute **<earthinstitute.columbia.edu/endofpoverty>**.

- ☐ Teach a child you know how to garden or arrange to visit a working farm that allows you to pick fruits and vegetables. Together appreciate the effort that goes into growing and harvesting food.

- ☐ Sign up for the Africa Bridge newsletter at **<africabridge.org>**.

- ☐ See chapter 22 for practical actions we can take to ensure plentiful water for all.

CONTRIBUTE

- ☐ Make a tax-deductible donation to TeleFood **<fao.org/food>** to help fund small, self-contained agriculture, livestock, and fisheries projects that help poor families produce more food by providing such things as seeds and tools. No money is spent on administrative costs.

- ☐ Encourage your elected government officials to support eco-friendly farming and protection of water resources.

- ☐ Donate to organizations contributing to sustainable agriculture and the well-being of small-farm families around the world, such as Millennium Promise **<millenniumpromise.org>**, Heifer **<heifer.org>**, World Neighbors **<wn.org>**, and CARE **<care.org>**.

"Our pride and joy"—that's how eleven-year-old Andrea Celeciana Semedo Da Veiga of Cape Verde in West Africa describes the school garden that supplies her and other students with fresh fruit and vegetables. The money for the seeds and the irrigation system came from the UN Food and Agriculture Organization's TeleFood program supported by contributions from people around the world **<fao.org/food>**. Andrea says, "We often spend time in our TeleFood garden. That's how I get to learn about growing things. I love working in the school garden." In addition to providing the children with lunch, a portion of the produce is sold to the local community and pays for meat, fish, and vegetables during the dry season, ensuring that the children can grow and flourish just like their garden.

☐ Help secure land rights. Support the work of the Rural Development Institute **<rdiland.org>**, a nonprofit organization that has helped secure land rights for more than 400 million people. On average every dollar contributed helps secure land ownership or ownerlike rights for nine people.

☐ Chip in to help provide tools for a family. KickStart **<kickstart.org>** is a nonprofit organization providing the tools and the technology, such as foot-operated irrigation pumps and oil presses, to help farmers in Africa start profitable, small-scale businesses. A $200 donation can provide the tools to help a family increase its income and escape poverty.

☐ Share part of your garden harvest with food pantries, community kitchens, and homeless shelters.

☐ Purchase food from local farmers' markets and food co-operatives.

SERVE

☐ Volunteer to support agricultural projects. Service trips can be arranged through Global Service Corps **<globalservicecorps.org>**, Voluntary Service Overseas **<vso.org.uk>**, and the International Volunteer Program Association **<volunteerinternational.org>**. Volunteers with the U.S. Agency for International Development's Farmer to Farmer program **<usaid.gov>** spend up to a month in a developing country, typically providing assistance to improve food production, processing, or marketing. Volunteers are not usually international development experts but rather retired people or others with farm or agribusiness experience.

> ***"We know what it would take to triple Africa's food yields, which are one-third of what other farmers in other parts of the world achieve. It requires improved seed...fertilizer or other soil nutrient inputs, and it requires water management technologies. This is not a high cost, but it is beyond the means of the poorest of the poor....It could be accomplished if we would stop saying no and roll up our sleeves and get to doing what we have committed to do."***
>
> — JEFFREY SACHS, DIRECTOR OF THE MILLENNIUM PROJECT

- ☐ Join with antihunger advocacy organizations to call for government aid programs to place a priority on the most pressing issues: support for local organizations; conservation and use of local-plant genetic resources; eco-friendly rural systems (including organic recycling, appropriate crop rotations, integrated soil nutrient management, and integrated pest/disease management); equitable access to natural resources and public service (including land, community pasture/forest, medicinal plants, water sources, and community irrigation water); and sustainable technologies (including animal power, seed, manure/fertilizers, and bio-pesticides).

- ☐ Observe International Migrants Day on December 18 by acquainting yourself with local migrant issues. Talk to migrant workers. Find out about their local housing and wages. Ask about their children.

- ☐ Read with older elementary children *Voices from the Field: Children of Migrant Farmworkers Tell Their Stories* by S. Beth Atkin and discuss what you can do to help.

☐ Start or support community organizations like New York City's Green Guerillas that develop community gardens. Help a park set up a garden as part of its recreation program. Work with a public housing project so that gardeners can grow food to eat or to generate income. Contact a local school and start a gardening project to "green" the school yard, produce food for students to share, and engage the students in learning more about food production.

LIVE

☐ Encourage others to understand and value sustainable agriculture.

☐ Purchase food grown by small family farms as much as possible. Visit the National Agricultural Library of the U.S. Department of Agriculture for information about community-supported agriculture **<nal.usda.gov>**.

☐ Join a community garden (or, if you don't have one, start one with friends). Mentor new gardeners and share your cuttings, produce, tools, and experience with others.

☐ Give thanks at mealtimes for those who grow our food.

Actions Make a Difference

After a severe 1995 flood in the African country of Burkina Faso, one fruit farmer, Claude Ariste, made a real difference. He invited fifteen other farmers to join him to create a farmer's cooperative, which has since grown into the National Fruit and Vegetable Growers' Federation of Burkina

Faso. Farmers are not only increasing their revenues through collaborative training, production, and marketing but their cooperative work enhances nutrition for farmers and communities and contributes to the reforestation of Sahelian (arid) zones. Not bad for one fruit farmer!

CHAPTER 7

Consume with Conscience

The [fortune-telling] tradition among the old campesinos is to turn their little cups over when they are finished. The future can be told from the dried stains left in the cup.... The future does depend on each cup, on each small choice we make.

— JULIA ALVAREZ,
A CAFECITO STORY

Let's Get a Cup of Coffee

It's amazing how much we get done over coffee. We share hot cups when we put our heads together with colleagues in a meeting or join a friend for a heart-to-heart; we balance cups as we drive to work or quietly sip as we visit with friends at the senior center.

With each cup we are connected to 236 million other Americans who also drink coffee. And by drinking it we're connected to all those people around the world who plant, tend, harvest, and sell it. Without our even realizing it, our choice of coffee has an impact on the lives of coffee growers: whether they can support their children or struggle to feed them, whether their land will be protected and productive or deforested and depleted.

By choosing socially responsible products and companies, we can help developing markets empower people. UN Millennium Development Goal 8 calls for global partnerships for development.

These days we have many more choices besides whether we drink our coffee black or with cream, *grande* or *venti*, decaf or caffeinated. We can choose whether the coffee we drink will contribute to eliminating poverty.

Consumption with a Conscience

We have choices for more than which coffee we drink. Stroll the supermarket aisles and read labels. You can select spaghetti sauce or salad dressing or popcorn from a company that donates all of its profits to fund programs for at-risk children. You can choose to buy a computer from a company that operates a foundation to improve global health. You can buy a car that pollutes less and may reduce our reliance on fossil fuels. When making informed furniture, clothing, toy, and craft purchases, you can be assured that the products were produced in an ethical, nonexploitive, and environmentally sound manner.

The bottom line doesn't mean what it used to. Many profitable companies now calculate success, in part, by how ethically their products are produced and/or by how their profits help others.

"One can buy anything with money except morality," wrote Jean Jacques Rousseau. Today we may not be able to buy morality, but we can exercise it in how we make and spend our money.

Imagine This...

"Are My Hands Clean?", a song by Sweet Honey in the Rock's Bernice Johnson Reagon, describes the journey of a blouse from its start as cotton in El Salvadoran fields through many other countries before winding up in a U.S. store. When you get dressed each day, look at the tags indicating where your garments were made. Picture the hands that worked on them. Find out about the labor practices of stores you frequent and then shop only at those with fair labor commitments.

Brewing Up a Better World

LEARN

- ☐ Invite a friend to join you for a cup of coffee and discuss how we can work to end poverty—at home and around the world.
- ☐ Explore **<globalenvision.org>** to learn more about the global economy and consider how we can make it work for everyone.
- ☐ Discover more about Fair Trade coffee and other issues from **<globalexchange.org>**, a Web site promoting social, economic, and environmental justice around the world.
- ☐ Host a Fair Trade movie night in your home or at your school, workplace, civic group, or place of worship. Screen the one-hour 2006 documentary *Buyer Be Fair: The Promise of Product Certification* **<buyerbefair.org>**. Serve Fair Trade coffee, tea, and other products. After the movie discuss how you can support Fair Trade, especially important when buying clothes, chocolate, and coffee.
- ☐ Visit **<sweatshopwatch.org>** and **<coopamerica.org>** to learn more about companies that produce and sell products produced without abusive labor practices.
- ☐ Suggest that your book club read *Collapse* by Jared Diamond and use the book as a springboard to discuss changing your consumption practices.

☐ Read with your family *A Cafecito Story* by Julia Alvarez; it tells of a young man's return to organic coffee production and how the authors also brought back songbirds.

CONTRIBUTE

☐ Purchase Fair Trade goods and products that are produced by socially responsible companies and encourage others, including your workplace and place of worship, to do so as well. Check out Co-op America **<coopamerica.org/programs/rs>** to find products and companies that support this mission.

☐ Support stores that provide markets and fair profits for craftspeople in developing countries, such as Ten Thousand Villages **<tenthousandvillages.com>**.

☐ Buy furniture that has FSC (Forest Stewardship Council) certification, assuring consumers that the indigenous people maintain control of their land and are fairly compensated for its use and that the lumber is removed in ways that conserve water and animal habitats and ensure other positive environmental impacts. Among others, IKEA **<ikea.com>**, Cotswold Furniture Makers **<cotswoldfurniture.com>**, and Charles Shackleton Furniture **<shackletonthomas.com>** carry FSC furniture.

☐ Before you adopt a favorite toy company, make sure the company complies with the global codes of conduct. You can check the list at **<toy-tia.org>**.

☐ Choose a credit card that makes donations to a charity based on the amount you charge on the card.

In **Oaxaca, Mexico,** residents ride a fleet of coffee cooperative–funded buses on routes that used to take hours to walk. In La Libertad, El Salvador, children who used to walk past an empty school building now study inside with a teacher who is paid by the coffee growers' cooperative. In Chajul, Guatemala, a coffee cooperative–funded health clinic is helping reduce child mortality. And in remote corners of Peru, growing numbers of children of uneducated farmers are pursuing university degrees, thanks in part to a predictable market for family-grown crops. Purchasing power and improved income can change the lives of coffee farmers and their communities. *Source:* **<www.time.com/time/insidebiz/article/0,9171,1139809,00.html>**

- ☐ Consider making purchases through for-profit Web sites such as **<benevolink.com>** that work with online businesses and contribute a percentage of the purchase price to the charity of your choice. Note that the contributions are not tax-deductible for the shopper; the businesses make the donation and take the deduction.

- ☐ Sign up for a supermarket program to donate money to local schools based on participants' purchases; designate a school with the greatest need to be the recipient even though it may not be your children's schools.

- ☐ Use "buy one, get one free" offers as a way of contributing at no extra cost to you. Donate the free item, whether it is a can of food or a pair of shoes, to an organization that serves people in your community who are in need.

SERVE

- ☐ Organize with others to urge local supermarkets and cafés to sell Fair Trade products. Give them informational materials available through **<transfairusa.org>** and **<globalexchange.org>**.

- ☐ Write a letter to the editor of your newspaper, celebrating ways people are finding to "buy smarter" and reuse more carefully.

- ☐ If you're a student, consider supporting the United Students for Fair Trade **<usft.org>**, a national student-led umbrella organization working to promote awareness and increase demand for Fair Trade products on university campuses. Organize a Trade Justice Day on campus.

- ☐ Connect with Business for Social Responsibility **<bsr.org>**, a nonprofit global organization that helps member companies achieve success in ways that respect ethical values, people, communities, and the environment. It provides information, tools, training, and advisory services to make corporate social responsibility an integral part of operations and strategies.

> ***"Whether they are teenagers buying Live Strong rubber bracelets, GenYers shopping for Fair Trade coffee, boomers waiting for hybrid vehicles, or retirees investing in socially responsible mutual funds, these consumers share one thing in common: a desire to spend money on products that align with their values."***
>
> — John Sage, co-founder and president of Pura Vida Coffee, special to the *Seattle Times*

- ☐ Coordinate an "alternative gifts" market for your place of worship during the holiday season. Make it easy for congregation members to purchase crafts produced by people in the developing world. The gifts available for purchase could also include suggested donations to organizations. Check out one of the many catalogs, such as World Vision's Gift Catalog **<greatgifts.org>**, for alternative gift ideas for many occasions.

LIVE

- ☐ Institute a family "buy nothing" day, week, or month to disengage from the consumer culture.

- ☐ Resolve that every time you or a family member buys something, you will give away a comparable item so that your home becomes gift-centered rather than accumulation-centered.

- ☐ Join the local business Chamber of Commerce branch that represents trade between your local region and foreign markets. By doing business with integrity, in a fair, honest, and lawful way, you will lead by example and encourage other businesspeople to treat their trading partners with respect and dignity.

- ☐ Read *Material World: A Global Family Portrait* by Peter Menzel, Charles C. Mann, and Paul Kennedy. Reflect on the amount of stuff in your life and what is necessary, sufficient, or excessive. What would be the benefits of a simpler lifestyle? Discuss spending choices, priorities, and values with family members. Determine the changes you will make.

☐ Commit to keeping usable but unwanted items out of the garbage dump and putting them into the hands of those who need them. Use a service like Freecycle **<freecycle.org>**.

Actions Make a Difference

Danny Grossman founded Wild Planet **<shopwildplanet.com>** to empower and inspire kids and to produce products that emphasize open-ended, nonviolent play. Grossman notes, "We learned early on that an ideal way to empower kids is to champion their ideas." Wild Planet launched a Kid Inventors' Challenge, purchased a company started by a nine-year-old, and produced the idea of a twelve-year-old who receives royalties to this day. Wild Planet sponsors an intern program for kids (especially those from at-risk populations), partners with kid-directed programs, and has been a leader in establishing and implementing a global code of conduct for manufacturing facilities to ensure that workers are treated well and especially to guard against the employment of children.

CHAPTER 8

Give from the Heart

More Thoughts on Giving

We make a living by what we get. We make a life by what we give.

— Sir Winston Churchill

Show Me the Money

We've all been there: You've just sat down to dinner when the phone rings. As the caller begins to speak, you hear other voices in the background and realize that it is another telemarketer calling. Or maybe you're sorting through mail from organizations seeking a donation. Our impulse is to be generous. Our deepest desire is to make a difference in the world. But how do we decide what to give and to whom?

To be sure, we have more to give than just our money: our compassionate concern, our time, our special talents, our voices calling for justice. But it is also true that how we use our money can contribute to making the world a better place. And that, in the now-familiar words of the credit card ad, is priceless.

Ten Questions to Consider When Selecting a Poverty-alleviating Organization for Donations

1. **What problems do you most want to solve?** What solutions excite you the most? Does the organization effectively address both the problem and the solutions? Does it work within an integrated understanding of and approach to eliminating poverty? (That is, even if the organization focuses on clean

water or education, does it recognize the other factors that affect poverty?)

2. **Whom does it help?** Do the organization's programs help those in greatest need?
3. **Does the organization align with your values?** If it is important to you, does the organization serve from a faith-based perspective? Is it committed to being inclusive? Does it operate without discrimination?
4. **Who runs the programs or projects funded by the organization?** Are international projects managed by staff from that country? Are U.S. programs guided by people from the local community?

"Rich people have always given money away. They've endowed libraries and things like that. The unique thing about this age is first of all you have a lot of people like Bill Gates and Warren Buffet who are interested in issues around the world that grow out of the nature of the twenty-first century and its inequalities—the income inequalities, the education inequalities, the health-care inequalities.... You get a guy like Gates who built Microsoft, and he actually believes that he can help overcome all of the health disparities in the world. That's the first thing. Second thing...there are a lot of people with average incomes who are joining me because of the Internet. Take the tsunami for example...we had $1.3 billion given...by households. The third thing is you have all these NGOs [non-government organizations] that you can partner with along with the government. So all these things together mean that people with real money want to give it away in ways that help people that before would've been seen only as the object of government grants or loans."

— President Bill Clinton, Fox News interview (September 24, 2006)

5. **Is it successful?** How does the organization measure its programs' success? How will the organization keep you informed about the difference that it and your contributions are making?

6. **What are the program's long-term prospects?** Does the organization have a broad or stable funding base? Is it expected to become self-supporting after the initial investment?

7. **Will it make good use of your donation?** Is the organization run efficiently and cost-effectively? Is no more than 15 percent of its budget spent on fund-raising and administration? Is it audited annually by an independent CPA firm? Request an annual report from the charity and/or consult **<charitynavigator.org>**, **<guidestar.org>**, **<charitywatch.org>**, and **<give.org>**. Ask your friends if they know more about the organization.

8. **How can you support it?** If it matters to you, beyond donating are there opportunities to volunteer, advocate, or inform and involve others?

9. **What is the organization's tax status?** If it matters to you, will your donation be tax-deductible? Avoid donating cash; checks and credit cards provide you with records and protection and can help ensure that your donation actually goes to the organization you intend to benefit.

10. **Is this the organization you think it is?** Look out for charities with similar-sounding names to ensure that you are giving to the one you intend to support. Less reputable outfits often take names similar to well-known and effective charities to mislead donors into thinking they are giving to the better-known charity.

Imagine This…

What if you doubled your charitable giving this year? What could you change in your daily life to be able to do that? What causes would you be excited about assisting? What difference do you imagine your contribution might make by the end of the year?

Giving Your Best

- ☐ Remember that, more than money, philanthropy takes heart.
- ☐ Listen to an audio recording of *Unleashing the Soul of Money: Find Sufficiency, Freedom, and Purpose—Through Your Relationship with Money* by Lynne Twist, available through **<amazon.com>**. Reflect on the place of money and philanthropy in your life.
- ☐ Explore your faith tradition's teachings about money, wealth, poverty, and compassionate giving. Christians will find resources at **<ministryofmoney.org>** to understand issues of money and faith in our lives, political systems, institutions, and world.
- ☐ Check with your employer about any matching programs for charitable donations and make the most of them.
- ☐ Give contributions to charities in lieu of gifts. For example, donate to Habitat for Humanity for a housewarming gift, provide sterile birthing kits in a developing country for a baby shower gift, or underwrite school fees for a child in a developing country for a graduation gift.
- ☐ Let guests know that for weddings or other gift-giving occasions you would prefer donations to a particular

charity. Online registries include **<idofoundation.org>** and **<justgive.org/weddings>**.

☐ Use an Internet search engine such as **<search.com>**, which donates half of its advertising revenue to charity. You can designate the charity of your choice.

☐ Explore Web sites such as Global Giving **<globalgiving.com>** that serve as clearinghouses for projects around the world that address a variety of social and environmental problems needing donations in a range of amounts. They will help you decide which charity would be a good fit for your contributions. There are many from which to choose. Use key words like *global health* or *poverty* to identify charities you might support among the 2,900 rated by Charity Navigator **<charitynavigator.org>**.

☐ Become more savvy about charities by visiting the National Charities Information Bureau **<give.org>**, Charity Watch **<charitywatch.org>**, and Charity Navigator **<charitynavigator.org>**. They will provide you with information on charitable organizations in an effort to help you make wise choices when giving.

☐ Sign up for automatic deductions to be made from your bank account to the charity of your choice.

☐ Commit to an organization for the long haul instead of changing charities frequently; doing so assists the charity with a steady donor base and deepens your connection to its work.

☐ Consider helping fund operations and infrastructure as well as programs; this is essential to organizations doing good work and it helps keep them going.

- ☐ Set a goal to increase by a certain amount the percentage of your family's disposable income given to charities to end global poverty.

- ☐ Contact your favorite international or domestic charity about putting a link from your Web site to its site to encourage visitors to your page to contribute to the charitable organization. Or put a search form for Universal Giving **<universalgiving.org>** on your Web site to encourage your visitors to donate to the international charities and causes you link them with through this straight (100 percent) pass-through service that channels donations to international organizations. Visit **<universalgiving.org/about_us>** and click on "Promote International Giving."

Actions to Take with Children

- ☐ Nurture children's awareness of giving as a basic facet of your family life and values. Explore the Learning to Give **<learningtogive.org>** resources for ideas. The extensive bibliography suggests many books for children of all ages, books that can stimulate discussion about giving, sharing, and caring. Encourage teachers and religious educators to use the resources for schools and places of worship too.

- ☐ If you give children an allowance, establish that one-third goes into a savings account, one-third is given to the charity of their choice, and one-third is theirs to spend.

- ☐ Involve family members in choosing a charity. Take time to talk about their interests, what problems stir their concern, and what solutions excite them. Family members may want to learn more about ending global poverty, investigate projects to support financially, and stay engaged through **<netaid.org>**, designed for young people.

When **Micah Daley-Harris** turned six, he hosted a Great American Bake Sale birthday party to raise money for Share Our Strength **<strength.org>**, a group that supports U.S. childhood hunger-prevention programs. Instead of birthday presents, each guest brought a batch of baked goods to sell at the bake sale stand set up at a neighborhood farmers' market. The children had a wonderful time, informed customers about childhood hunger, raised several hundred dollars, and tasted the sweet satisfaction of helping other kids.

- ☐ Use holidays like Thanksgiving and Hanukkah to give children or grandchildren a financial gift with a requirement that they contribute or invest it in three nonprofits. At the end of the timeline (especially fun if it is another holiday or special occasion), have them tell to whom they gave the money and why.

- ☐ Ask children to plan birthday parties oriented around a concern they care about, and encourage contributions to help the charity in lieu of gifts.

- ☐ Help children identify ways to raise money to contribute by doing something they enjoy, such as coaching younger children in a weekend soccer clinic or making and selling friendship bracelets.

- ☐ Hold a family conference to decide what expenses you can cut so that you can contribute the money to a poverty-ending organization, which might be linked to the family change. (For instance, if your family decides to stop buying bottled water and drink tap water instead, you could contribute the saved money to an organization providing clean water to communities in sub-Saharan Africa.)

- ☐ Plan an annual celebration that affirms the impact of your giving. For example, if you sponsor a child in a developing country, have a party on the child's birthday and talk about the things the child has been able to do over the past year because of your contribution.

- ☐ Watch *Baraka* (1994) with your family and friends and discuss how we might give from a sense of gratitude for our beautiful planet and all its wonderful faces. *Baraka* is a Sufi word for something similar to "breath of life" or "blessing." Director Ron Fricke uses images and sound gathered from twenty-four countries to create a stunning collage of life, which he has called a "guided meditation."

Actions Make a Difference

Adam Roberts was frustrated. While attending a conference on world poverty, he was still left wondering, *What can one person do?* He decided to start The $10 Club **<thetendollarclub.org>**, inviting others to join him in contributing $10 every month to a meaningful poverty-alleviating project somewhere in the world. Now, just a few years later, his $10 Club is incorporated as a small nonprofit with three hundred members who give $36,000 annually. Notes member Anne Mesnikoff, "Adam donates his time (he also has a full-time job) and does the research to find the places where the U.S. dollar will make the most difference in the lives of individuals living in the kind of poverty we can't comprehend." Referring to the Jewish concept of repairing the world, she says, "There are few things in my experience that embody *Tikkun Olam* more."

PART II

Afternoon

CHAPTER 9

End Hunger and Malnutrition

When I feed the poor, they call me a saint. When I ask why the poor have no food, I am called a Communist.

— THE LATE ARCHBISHOP DOM HÉLDER CÂMARA OF RECIFE, BRAZIL

What's for Lunch?

Eliot and his colleague sat down at a restaurant table for a business lunch. The colleague scanned the menu, made his choice, and waited for Eliot to decide. Eliot scrutinized the choices, he debated which sounded better, he sighed with the difficulty of the decision, he went back and forth between two options, and he groaned about having to choose. Finally, his colleague leaned over, put his hand on Eliot's arm, and said, "Eliot, it's only lunch."

Instead of wrestling with menu choices, let's spend our energy grappling with the question that really matters: what can *we* do to end hunger? In the United States, 35 million Americans, including one in five children, live in households that are "food insecure," a horribly cold term that means they struggle to put food on the table, they eat less nutritious food because it is cheaper, or they are just not getting enough to eat. Around the world more than 852 million children and adults are hungry or malnourished. What actions can we take to bring an end to this unconscionable situation?

Together we can end the hidden hunger of chronic malnutrition and meet UN Millennium Development Goal 1 of eradicating extreme hunger and poverty, with a target of reducing by half by 2015 the proportion of people who suffer from hunger.

Hunger has many causes and calls for many kinds of responses, from simple to complex. Often some very minimal help creates the opportunity for people to generate income, grow food, or raise livestock so they have enough food that they can count on day to day. In developing countries better seeds, a well, irrigation systems, agricultural know-how, or microcredit can make all the difference. In developed countries like the United States, job training, a living wage, and affordable housing, child care, health care, and transportation are keys. Other solutions call for local and national partnerships. Read on for the menu of actions you can take.

Imagine This...

The Thrifty Food Plan serves as the basis for food-stamp calculations—representing the cost deemed sufficient to prepare adequate, nutritious meals. For example, a family of four (two adults and two children under five, in this case) is supposed to be able to eat a nutritionally sound diet for $102.30 a week, which comes to $1.21 per meal per person. These guidelines assume that a family will have access to the cheapest bulk food items (including fresh produce), will have the time and the tools for labor-intensive preparation, and won't use convenience foods.

Look carefully at your most recent grocery receipts. Could you feed your family on the Thrifty Food Plan? Now imagine that you lack transportation, work multiple jobs per day, and live in a community without convenient, lower-cost supermarkets. How much harder do you think it would be to feed your family? What if you presented your congressional representatives with the challenge of living on the Thrifty Food Plan for a month?

Taking Action to End Hunger in Our Nation and the World

LEARN

☐ Visit Web sites of organizations working to end hunger both in the United States and around the world. Bread for the World's "Links to Other Anti-Hunger and Poverty Organizations" portal at **<bread.org/learn/links.html>** is an excellent starting point.

☐ Watch movies about hunger and poverty with your family and friends and talk about what you've learned. Here are four from the Librarian and Information Science News **<http://movies.lisnews.org>**: *City of God* (2002), *Mother India* (1957), *The Gleaners and I* (2000), and *Mother Teresa: In the Name of God's Poor* (1997).

☐ Organize events for National Hunger Awareness Day coordinated by America's Second Harvest **<secondharvest.org>** to help others in your community learn more about hunger and how they can act.

☐ See chapters 1, 3, and 6 for more actions to reduce acute hunger and increase incomes and food production.

CONTRIBUTE

- ☐ Pack brown bag lunches with nutritious, nonperishable food items (such as energy bars, nuts, juice boxes, water bottles, and dried fruit) and keep them in your car or take a few with you when you run errands. Or get vouchers from local food pantries and community kitchens to give away. If you are approached by a homeless person for spare change, you can provide more-substantial and nutritious help.

- ☐ Make a donation to CARE **<care.org>** to support agricultural and natural resource projects that focus on agricultural production (such as crops, livestock, and soil management), post-harvest handling (such as processing, storage, and marketing), and natural resource conservation (such as protecting soil and water quality).

- ☐ Give the cost of a farm animal through Heifer Project International **<heifer.org>** to help a hungry family in the developing world receive livestock, training, and other services. They will benefit from the food and the income the livestock provides and will pay it forward by giving the offspring to other families.

SERVE

- ☐ Help eligible people learn about and enroll for Food Stamps and WIC, the Special Supplemental Nutrition Program for Women, Infants, and Children. The debit cards and vouchers can be used only for food and effectively reduce hunger. The Food and Nutrition Service of the U.S. Department of Agriculture **<fns.usda.gov/fns/outreach.htm>** has ideas and materials to help congregations, community groups, and individuals

D**octors routinely saw** stunted, apathetic children with swollen stomachs, dull eyes, and poorly healing wounds characteristic of malnutrition. Where did these children live? In the Mississippi Delta, Appalachia, coastal areas of South Carolina, and other parts of the United States as recently as the 1960s. But no more. What made the difference? A field team of doctors found that there wasn't an overall improvement in living standards or a decrease of joblessness in these areas. Rather they credited the advent of Food Stamps, Head Start, school lunch and breakfast programs, and the Special Supplemental Nutrition Program for Women, Infants, and Children (WIC) with putting an end to extreme childhood hunger and malnutrition in the United States.

assist with outreach. Use your outreach experience to become a strong advocate for adequate funding of these important programs. (See chapter 24 for more advocacy ideas.)

☐ Ensure that your community provides free school breakfasts and summer meals through the National School Lunch Program **<fns.usda.gov/cnd/lunch>** so that hungry children can count on a solid meal each day. If your community doesn't provide summer meals, help arrange a host site so that it can.

☐ Volunteer, perhaps with a friend, to deliver Meals on Wheels **<mowaa.org>** to senior citizens on fixed incomes and people who are homebound. Or commit to looking in on an elderly or homebound neighbor and provide a meal to share. If your place of worship has a van, see if there are senior citizens in the community who need transportation to the grocery store or to meals at a senior center or community center.

☐ Join an advocacy organization that works on domestic and global hunger, such as Bread for the World **<bread.org>** and RESULTS **<results.org>**, for partners, information, training, and support in making your voice heard on policies to end world hunger. Speaking out together, we can work for long-term, systemic change and greater justice. And we don't have to go it alone!

- ☐ Work with a community group to set up a volunteer transportation program to help low-income people from urban neighborhoods or rural communities make weekly trips to full-sized, well-stocked supermarkets. Petition grocery chains to open stores in underserved areas.

- ☐ Support the establishment of weekly farmers' markets in urban communities to provide access to fresh produce and to support local farmers.

- ☐ Organize parents and others to demand healthy and nutritious food for schools, camps, and child-care and after-school programs. Replace soda and junk food with healthy options. Encourage a curriculum that teaches children to make smart nutritional choices and to see through junk food advertising aimed at them.

- ☐ Involve students in the National Student Campaign Against Hunger and Homelessness **<nscahh.org>**, an organization dedicated to educating, engaging, and training students for direct service and advocacy.

LIVE

- ☐ At every mealtime remember those without enough to eat.

- ☐ Model and teach healthy food choices to the children and others in your life.

Actions Make a Difference

Sasha Earnheart-Gold, a California teenager, took an educational tour through Tibet and Nepal. "Every day I saw starving children with bone-thin arms and bloated stomachs." Then he visited a village that was full of huge apple trees, where no one seemed hungry. An idea was planted. Sasha turned to home-schooling mentors to help him create the nonprofit Apple Tree Foundation and raise an initial $5,000—enough to start 1,200 apple trees. Less than a year later, Sasha and his Apple Tree International team were in Bolivia and Nepal, where scores of eager townspeople came to their grafting workshops and agreed to teach at least one other person, creating a ripple effect. In seven years Sasha and Apple Tree International have overseen the planting of thousands of trees and taught sustainable practices to hundreds of people. Next up for Apple Tree: funding local nurseries in impoverished regions. "Even as small an action as bringing some apple trees to a community is important." *Source: Ode* (October 2005)

CHAPTER 10

Extend the Reach of Technology

All things are connected. Whatever befalls the earth befalls the children of the earth. We do not weave the web of life, we are merely a strand in it. Whatever we do to the web, we do to ourselves.

— Chief Sealth (Seattle), Suquamish leader

Making the Connection

Can you imagine not being able to pick up the phone to call someone or to get on the computer to send an e-mail or instantly access the vast amounts of knowledge and information on the Internet? Whether it's instant messaging or text messaging, e-mail or voicemail, search engines or RSS feeds, many of us are able to immediately connect to people and information virtually anywhere in the world. Accessing information and communicating with others is an essential part of our daily lives. Still far too many people have yet to make their first telephone call let alone use a computer or access the Internet.

Technology can connect people with one another and expand opportunities for income, education, and more. UN Millennium Development Goal 8—develop a global partnership for development—includes a target of making available the benefits of new technologies, especially information and communication technologies, in cooperation with the private sector.

But in many developing countries, an information and communications technology revolution is marching forward, village by village. The revolutionaries include two hundred thousand "village phone ladies" from Bangladesh to Uganda, who earn a living selling cell phone time to rural community members who would otherwise have no phone access; and slum residents in the Philippines can now buy affordable food over text-messaging networks. Many children in the United States and other countries who cannot afford new computers are learning technology skills with the help of donated, refurbished computers.

A Network of Mutuality

Technology offers great promise as an important tool for easing and ending poverty, providing more and better opportunities for people to integrate into the mainstream economy, expanding access to markets, and linking people to wider job opportunities. It connects more of us to information, education, skills training, and services. Technology increases productivity, saves time and money, provides greater safety, and gives less advantaged people a stronger voice in the world beyond their village. Information and knowledge help level the playing field, allowing people to lift themselves and their families out of poverty.

> *"All life is interrelated...tied in a single garment of destiny. Whatever affects one directly, affects all indirectly....I can never be what I ought to be until you are what you ought to be. You can never be what you ought to be until I am what I ought to be....This is the interrelated structure of reality."*
>
> — Dr. Martin Luther King Jr.

The global interconnectedness we now experience through the use of a multitude of technologies reminds us that we are indeed caught, to use Dr. King's words, in an "inescapable network of mutuality." Each action we take to help people around the world communicate and connect will, in the end, help us all.

Imagine This…

Consider some of the personal ways that you are already "connected" to people from many other countries: through the food you eat (where it was produced or the origin of the recipe); the clothes you wear; the toys, games, and sports equipment you enjoy; and our immigrant ancestry. Now imagine new ways to *personally* connect to people and help end poverty via technology: business mentoring via satellite phone, sharing medical knowledge via e-mail or videoconference, and sharing knowledge in virtual classrooms over the Internet. In what new and creative ways can technology be used to help end poverty?

Answering the Call

LEARN

☐ Investigate and inform yourself about the benefits, as well as the limitations, of technology in solving poverty issues. To learn more about the appropriate uses of technology in developing countries, visit **<globalenvision.org>**. This organization strives to provide a balanced presentation of information from multiple perspectives and opinions regarding many of the relevant issues related to globalization.

☐ Visit the Web site of your favorite high-tech company and learn about the nonprofit programs it may be partnering with and supporting.

- ☐ Get inspired by the future of creative technology-based solutions to address many of humanity's most pressing problems. The Tech Museum Awards **<techawards.org>** is an international awards program that honors innovators from around the world who apply technology to benefit humanity.

- ☐ Read *The World Is Flat* by Thomas Friedman for a perspective on the new connectedness of our global community and the role that technology advances have played in bringing us all closer together.

- ☐ Sign up for Really Simple Syndication (RSS) feeds to receive ongoing updates via blogs and news feeds on what's happening with different poverty initiatives. Ones you might want to check out include **<yellowbrix.com>**, **<news.yahoo.com>**, and **<nytimes.com/services/xml/rss>**.

SERVE

- ☐ Offer to put your basic computer skills to use by teaching introductory computer classes for nonprofits in your community. Or, if your technical skill is more advanced, offer your services as a volunteer consultant. **<npower.org>** is a national nonprofit network that offers a variety of technology assistance to other nonprofit organizations so that they can become more efficient with their already-limited resources.

- ☐ Blogs such as **<sowhatcanIdo.blogspot.com>** are a great way to find and share ideas with others who are also interested in discovering ways to help solve poverty-related problems.

Eight hundred schools in Rwanda are running laptops on solar power. The idea came from the British company Digital Links **<digital-links.org>**, which has already sent more than fifty thousand secondhand computers to developing countries. Solar cells were hooked up to the computers in cooperation with Solarcentury **<solarcentury.com>**. Jeremy Leggett of Solarcentury says it is a unique chance to show what solar cells can do.

- ☐ If you have the skills, design a Web site for a poverty-related organization or do other types of "virtual volunteer" work.
- ☐ If you enjoy writing, write for organizations and serve people's needs from your own home. Many nonprofits need help with writing newsletters, proposals, and grants as well as other tasks that can be done via computer.
- ☐ Answer phones for a nonprofit's hotline or ask what other help the organization may need. Check the local phone directory for community service organizations or crisis hotlines or do a search on the Internet.

CONTRIBUTE

- ☐ Click for a cause. Use your computer and Internet connection to visit the Web site of at least one organization with a button to click that will generate a donation. For example, each click on the Hunger Site **<thehungersite.com>**, which supports the hunger relief efforts of Mercy Corps **<mercycorps.org>** and America's Second Harvest **<secondharvest.org>**, provides 1.1 cups of staple food. When you click at **<theliteracysite.com>**, the Literacy Site buys books for children through its partner, First Book **<firstbook.org>**.

☐ Apply your computing power to research. Your computer's unused "brainpower" accessed over the Internet can work to solve many challenging global problems, including improved treatment for HIV/AIDS. To learn how visit **<worldcommunitygrid.org>**.

☐ Donate your older (but still working) computer to an organization that refurbishes computers and then distributes them to individuals or organizations that need them. Some places to start include Gifts in Kind **<giftsinkind.org>**, the Salvation Army **<salvationarmyusa.org>**, Goodwill **<goodwill.org>**, Computers for Schools **<pcsforschools.org>**, World Computer Exchange **<worldcomputerexchange.org>**, and the National Cristina Foundation **<cristina.org>**.

☐ Start a drop-box program to collect old cell phones for donation to domestic violence shelters and other programs serving people in need for use in emergencies.

LIVE

☐ Volunteer your computer skills to help teach others in developing countries. For example, Geekcorps **<geekcorps.org>** is a U.S.-based, nonprofit organization that places international technical volunteers to contribute to information and communications technology (ICT) projects while transferring the technical skills required to achieve long-term stability through the benefits of modern telecommunications.

☐ Discover new ways that you can use technology to save time and money in your own life; then use those additional resources to be of service in your own community.

Actions Make a Difference

Students from San José State University are using computer maps to help people living in poorer neighborhoods. The professor who envisioned this project, Malu Roldan, said, "The community is our textbook." The students started in the spring of 2005, using pocket PCs, GPS receivers, and digital cameras to survey nineteen underserved San Jose neighborhoods. Then students created scalable maps of the district and a menu for specifying residential mixed use of green space; they then created data fields for such components as bike lanes, traffic lights, sidewalks, trails, and even graffiti. As a result, one community, Five Wounds/Brookwood Terrace, will have new streetlights, sidewalks, and traffic signals. By 2008 it will also have 17 acres of parkland. Begun as a class project, this effort shows communities how business groups, faith-based organizations, neighborhood coalitions, nonprofit groups, schools, and local residents can come together to create better living space for their neighbors. *Source:* Thomas Ulrich, "How Computer Maps Will Help the Poor," *Christian Science Monitor* (October 12, 2005), **<csmonitor.com/2005/1012/p13s02-legn.html>**

CHAPTER 11

Expand Access to Microcredit

You know that mantra, "Give a man a fish, he'll eat for a day. Teach a man to fish, he'll eat for a lifetime"? It's missing something: microfinance is the fishing rod, the boat, the net, etc. Cash and dignity, side by side....Maybe the mantra should be: "Give a man a fish, he'll eat for a day. Give a woman microcredit, she, her husband, her children, and her extended family will eat for a lifetime."

— BONO, LEAD SINGER OF U2 AND GLOBAL ADVOCATE

Saving the World

Do you remember your first bank account? Maybe it was a savings account your parents helped you open when you were a child so you could deposit a birthday check or your allowance; the little savings book seemed so grown-up. Maybe your first bank account wasn't a childhood landmark but marked a transition to greater independence as you opened a first account at college, preparing to live away from home for the first time. Or was your first bank account a place to put the wages from your first job?

Millions of very poor people in the United States and around the world will never forget their first bank account as they gain access to small amounts of credit and banking services, known as microcredit or microfinance. With a tiny loan, they can start small businesses and profit from their own hard work, whether rice husking or house cleaning, weaving cloth or providing child care.

Microcredit turns banking upside down, making it available to those who are often the poorest and traditionally excluded. Whereas most banks lend only large sums, microcredit institutions provide small loans. Whereas banks require a lot of paperwork, microfinance institutions make loans to people who cannot read or write. Whereas banks lend mostly to those who are literate, microfinance institutions make loans to people who cannot read. In developing countries, instead of borrowers making an arduous journey to the bank, microcredit staff travel to the villages; and instead of loans going mostly to men, women compose the majority of microborrowers. As a result of this banking revolution, millions of the world's poorest people are working their way out of poverty, starting their own businesses and able to feed their families, build adequate housing, and keep their children in school.

Microcredit enables people to profit from their work and leave poverty behind. It can help us meet Millennium Development Goal 1 of eradicating extreme hunger and poverty and its target for 2015 of reducing by half the proportion of people who earn less than $1 a day.

Imagine This...

Imagine what your life would be like without access to financial services. How could you go to college without a loan? Could you even purchase a car? How could you buy or fix up a house without a mortgage? Not to mention your retirement. Where would you be without the ability to save and earn interest or without the ability to invest?

Making a Big Difference with Small Change

LEARN

- ☐ Read a book to learn more about microcredit, such as *Banker to the Poor* by Muhammad Yunus, *Give Us Credit* by Alex Counts, *The Price of a Dream* by David Bornstein, and *Kitchen Table Entrepreneurs: How Eleven Women Escaped Poverty and Became Their Own Bosses* by Martha Shirk and Anna S. Wadia. Recommend the reading to others as well through your book group or other group.

- ☐ Read the *Grameen Dialogue*, an online newsletter **<grameen-info.org/dialogue>**. Or subscribe to microfinance publications, such as the *Economic and Social Rights Review*, to obtain cutting-edge information on microfinance.

- ☐ To learn more about microcredit, watch Charlie Rose's interview with Muhammad Yunus (order episodes aired on September 20, 2005, and June 4, 2004, through **<charlierose.com>**). Invite friends to watch with you, or arrange to show it at your school, workplace, civic group, or place of worship.

- ☐ Visit the Web site of a microfinance institution to learn more about its work and how you can support it. You can link to microfinance institutions around the world through the Microcredit Summit Campaign **<microcreditsummit.org>**. Also learn about the World Bank's Consultative Group on Assisting the Poor's work to promote microcredit **<cgap.org>**.

- ☐ Download the *State of the Microcredit Summit Campaign Report* from **<microcreditsummit.org>**. Also read *Enhancing Opportunities for Entrepreneurship* and *Enhancing Economic Opportunity Through Entrepreneurship* from **<ms.foundation.org>**; click on "Publications & Reports," then "Program Publications."

- ☐ Subscribe to *Microfinance Matters* **<uncdf.org/mfmatters>**, a monthly Web publication from United Nations Capital Development Fund.

- ☐ Learn more about children's savings accounts, which are seeded at birth for everyone and then matched for lower-income children. Visit **<assetbuilding.org>**, **<childsavingsinternational.org>**, and the Corporation for Enterprise Development **<cfed.org>**.

Muhammad Yunus is the founder and the managing director of the Grameen Bank in Bangladesh and the 2006 recipient of the Nobel Peace Prize. In the early 1970s, with a PhD in economics from Vanderbilt University, Yunus returned to Bangladesh to teach at Chittagong University. During a severe famine, he went into the village next to his campus to see if he could be of help to even one person. There, Yunus met Sophia Khatoon, who earned only $0.02 profit for a long day's work making bamboo stools. She didn't have the money to buy the bamboo, so she had to borrow the money from a trader on the condition that she sell the finished product back to him at a price he set. His price barely covered the cost of the bamboo, leaving her with a two-penny return on her hard work.

Yunus found forty-one others who borrowed from the same trader and needed a total of $27 to free themselves from this debt trap. The money Yunus lent them in 1976 averaged $0.68 each. Khatoon's profits soared from $0.02 per day to $1.25 because she could now sell the stools to the highest bidder. They were the first borrowers of Grameen Bank, which now has 7 million borrowers in Bangladesh, 95 percent of whom are women.

☐ Visit a microfinance institution to meet microentrepreneurs and to witness firsthand the impact of microcredit. Such trips are coordinated by ACCION **<accion.org>**, FINCA **<villagebanking.org>**, Global Partnerships **<globalpartnerships.org>**, Katalysis Bootstrap Fund **<katalysis.org>**, Unitus **<unitus.com>**, and others. Invite a journalist or the local TV station to accompany you. When you return, address your religious, civic, or other group and write an article for the newspaper or for newsletters of organizations to which you belong.

CONTRIBUTE

☐ Appreciate the importance of banking services and help extend them to others. When you pay bills, include a check to a microcredit program.

☐ Make a donation to the Calvert Foundation's Community Giftshares Program **<calvertfoundation.org>**. Your gift will be put to use in a revolving loan fund that provides financing to organizations working for people who are poor.

☐ Purchase goods produced by microentrepreneurs. Visit **<projectenterprise.org/member_directory/index.htm>**, **<planfund.org/business_directory.html>**, and **<worldofgood.com>** for sources.

☐ Host a dinner party where guests can learn about microcredit and are invited to write a check to underwrite a new microcredit program. Identify potential recipients by contacting such groups as Freedom from Hunger **<freedomfromhunger.org>**, Kiva **<kiva.org>**, Opportunity International **<opportunity.org>**, and others listed in this chapter.

- ☐ Invite your children to make a piggybank for the family's spare change at the end of the day (and an agreed-upon portion of the children's allowance). Monthly, send a check for the accumulated change to a microcredit program.

- ☐ Match the savings of low-income people using individual development accounts—matched savings accounts for first homes, business ownership (microenterprise), higher education and training, or retirement savings. Through five hundred such programs, anyone can match the savings of low-income people, who may use the savings only for the specified purposes and must participate in appropriate financial education.

SERVE

- ☐ Advocate that legislators and institutions such as U.S. Agency for International Development **<usaid.gov>** and the World Bank **<worldbank.org>** include microcredit programs reaching the very poor as core elements of their strategies to end poverty. Connect with an advocacy organization such as RESULTS **<results.org>** for resources and support.

- ☐ Support a microcredit program in your community or start one. Visit the Association for Enterprise Opportunity at **<microenterpriseworks.org>** to find a microcredit program near you. Consider serving on the board.

- ☐ Work through the appropriate channels of your religious congregation to encourage its investment in microcredit funds, such as the Shefa Fund, Oikocredit, the Common Good Fund, the Calvert Foundation, and the Opportunity Finance Network. (Shefa and Calvert both allow low minimums.)

- ☐ Be a mentor. Use your skills and talent to train, support, and educate a small-business startup in your community through a microcredit program.

- ☐ Start a blog. Open a dialogue on microcredit issues via blog chat rooms with photographs, anecdotes, and suggestions.

LIVE

- ☐ Invest some of your money in a microcredit-financing institution like Oikocredit **<oikocredit.org>** or the Katalysis Bootstrap Fund **<katalysis.org>**. Although you won't earn the highest possible monetary returns, you will earn modest interest while enabling the very poor to participate in more microcredit programs. Or go to **<communityinvest.org>** and **<calvertfoundation.org>** to look up the names of more than thirty microfinance organizations in which you or your group can invest.

Actions Make a Difference

When the Microcredit Summit Campaign was launched in 1997, microloans were reaching only 7.6 million very poor families worldwide. By 2005 that number jumped to 82 million, benefiting 410 million family members. The campaign's second phase now seeks by 2015 to reach 175 million borrowers and ensure that 100 million families rise above the $1-a-day threshold, lifting 500 million people out of extreme poverty.

CHAPTER 12

Encourage Social Entrepreneurship

We need to remember that we are all created creative and can invent new scenarios as frequently as they are needed.

— MAYA ANGELOU, AMERICAN AUTHOR AND POET

Aiming High

The year is 1961, and John F. Kennedy is early in his presidency. Although space exploration has just begun, President Kennedy declares an ambitious—and, to many, unattainable—vision: to put a person on the moon before the end of the decade. Astonishingly, with commitment, persistence, and resources, we achieved it.

The UN Millennium Development Goals set out today's "moon shot." Retired Republican senator Mark Hatfield of Oregon reflected, "We stand by as children starve by the millions because we lack the will to eliminate hunger. Yet we have found the will to develop missiles capable of flying over the polar cap and landing within a few hundred feet of their target. This is not innovation. It is a profound distortion of humanity's purpose on earth." How can we foster positive innovation to fulfill our highest purpose?

Social entrepreneurs are creating new ways to solve our world's most serious social problems, which will help us reach the UN Millennium Development Goals.

Thinking Outside the Box

Ending global poverty in our day will require the best creative thinking we can muster. The way it has always been approached—the conventional wisdom of "the same old, same old"—has not spurred the change that is needed. If we are going to create a new future for our world, it is time to think in new ways.

> *"I am convinced that poor people are just as human as anyone else. They have just as much potential as anyone. They are simply shoved into a box marked POOR! And it's written in giant letters so that everyone simply treats them the way poor people are treated, because we think this is the way we should treat them. This means it isn't easy to get out of the box."*
>
> — Muhammad Yunus, founder and managing director, Grameen Bank, Bangladesh

Across the globe social entrepreneurs are demonstrating the power of new ideas to effect change. Their innovative solutions can solve our most urgent social problems.

It is time to apply all of our creative energy, imagination, inspired dreams, and deepest hopes—and support other out-of-the-box thinkers. Together we can tear open the box marked *POOR!* and free the potential of all who have been shoved into it for so long.

Imagine This...

Do you have what it takes to dream big and make a difference? Imagine some positive change that you actually could put into place. Can you see it? *Really* see it? You might not know the specifics just yet, but if you can see the dream, you can figure out whom to enlist to help you fulfill your dream.

Turning Dreams into Reality

LEARN

- ☐ Grab a pen and paper. Take a few moments and reflect on any thoughts you have that work *against* an end to poverty. Make a list of phrases you keep hearing: *It's hopeless. Governments are corrupt. The poor will always be with you. There's not enough to go around. We keep sending them money and nothing changes.* Set these phrases aside as you open yourself up to a creative rethinking process.

- ☐ List your five greatest talents and your five greatest passions. What ignites your mind and heart? What gives you fulfillment? Think as broadly as possible about how you might use, or might already be using, those talents and passions to work toward the end of poverty. Dream big.

- ☐ Read *How to Change the World: Social Entrepreneurs and the Power of New Ideas* by David Bornstein, which profiles people whose visions for improving the world have become reality, affecting the lives of millions.

> ***"Rather than leaving societal needs to the government or business sectors, social entrepreneurs find what is not working and solve the problem by changing the system, spreading the solution, and persuading entire societies to take new leaps. They are both visionaries and ultimate realists, concerned with the practical implementation of their vision above all else."***
>
> — Ashoka, a global association of social entrepreneurs <ASHOKA.ORG>

- ☐ Visit the Web site of the Ashoka Foundation **<ashoka.org>** to learn more about social entrepreneurs and read about Ashoka Fellows in the news. Sign up for its quarterly newsletter for more information.
- ☐ Watch *The New Heroes: Their Bottom Line Is Lives,* a four-part PBS series profiling social entrepreneurs.
- ☐ Visit a social enterprise and learn about it firsthand.

Recognizing the important role the education system plays in creating and reinforcing gender disparities in every facet of Egyptian society, Magdy Aziz, a 2005 Ashoka Fellow, is tackling discrimination from the bottom up: he's teaching elementary school children what their rights are and should be—and how to demand that those rights be respected. Through "rights of the child" groups in elementary schools, Aziz is introducing children to international and national conventions that govern rights and is giving them a safe space to practice exercising those rights in ways that can transfer to their lives outside of school.

By encouraging boys and girls alike to contribute ideas and take on leadership roles, the groups foster not only gender equality but also political and community participation skills in what is traditionally a very rigid school system. In this environment children are able to take ownership of their rights and, by enforcing them among their peers, become messengers for them.

To ensure that the lessons learned in school are reinforced in the home and spread to the larger community, Aziz created school committees that provide a direct link between teachers and parents. Higher-level consultative committees of decision-makers at the local and national levels then help spread the ideas to other schools, education levels, and government institutions. Aziz is also working with parents and government officials to promote the implementation of laws to protect children's rights and prohibit gender discrimination. *Source:* **<ashoka.org>**

> ***"One of the great equalizing factors of social entrepreneurship is that the great social entrepreneurs are not the geniuses of society. They are not the best educated or the richest or the most talented. Rather, they tend to be the people who are the most strongly motivated in a particular area.…People are great social entrepreneurs when they are very clear and very driven to bring about the positive social change that they want to bring. Most of the things they need to know, they learn along the way. Or they bring in people who can do things that they're not good at."***
>
> — DAVID BORNSTEIN, *HOW TO CHANGE THE WORLD: SOCIAL ENTREPRENEURS AND THE POWER OF NEW IDEAS*

CONTRIBUTE

☐ Invest in the work of the Ashoka Foundation to support the development of social entrepreneurs. Explore options for supporting their work financially.

☐ Support young people in dreaming big and making a difference in our world. Youth Venture **<youthventure.org>** helps empower young people ages twelve to twenty by providing them with all the tools necessary to create civic-minded organizations, clubs, and businesses. A venture can be any youth-created, youth-led organization designed to provide a positive lasting benefit in a school, neighborhood, or community. Youth Venture provides access to a variety of resources, including a national network of like-minded young people, media opportunities, and up to $1,000 in seed capital to launch a venture. Do Something **<dosomething.org>** provides $500 grants to young people who want to make a difference.

SERVE

- ☐ Offer to serve as a coach to someone starting a new business or social change enterprise.
- ☐ Lend your professional skills—marketing, writing, consulting, or whatever—to the venture of a social entrepreneur.
- ☐ Volunteer with a social change enterprise at home or abroad.

LIVE

- ☐ Keep a journal and spin out your dream of what you would like to accomplish this month, this year, and in your lifetime. Focus on the change you want to effect in the world. Identify problems, brainstorm solutions, and list ideas and resources. Make plans. Develop a timeline.

Actions Make a Difference

Shree Padre, one of Ashoka's 1,800 Fellows, is a rainwater harvest specialist in India. He explains, "I just study the various indigenous methods adopted by our intelligent farmers, many of whom are illiterate, to conserve water, harvest rainwater, dry-land farm, and save water in various parts across the country; document them; and disseminate the information to other needy farmers. There are wonderful stories around the country to inspire thousands of people." Padre's work to share the information through slideshows, articles, books, and other methods is helping countless others capture not just life-giving water but also life-sustaining inspiration.

CHAPTER 13

Ensure Health Care for All

Health is a state of complete physical, mental and social well-being, and not merely the absence of disease or infirmity.

— Constitution, the World Health Organization

Health. Care.

"You look really awful!" Perhaps the only time we welcome these words is when they are not a superficial criticism of an outfit or a bad haircut but instead an expression of real concern if we're sick. In our "how-are-you-I'm-fine" culture, what a relief that someone notices and cares!

Whether we do something as simple as helping a loved one crawl between cool sheets, sip something soothing, and fall into needed sleep, or whether it involves taking a friend to the doctor and filling a prescription, our genuine concern and our determined actions do make a difference.

For a strong future, everyone needs and deserves good health care. UN Millennium Development Goal 6 calls on us to combat HIV/AIDS, malaria, and other diseases.

Now is the time to broaden our expressions of care to encompass others. What looks "really awful" is the pain on the faces of our nation's 46.6 million people without health insurance, who may be unable to see a doctor when they need to and who face a mountain of medical debt when they do. They live sicker and die younger than Americans with health insurance. What looks "really awful" are our world's inaction and lack of prevention and treatment as reflected in the gaunt faces of 3 million sisters and brothers who are dying of AIDS each year; the heaving chests of 2 million tuberculosis (TB) patients gasping for their last breaths; the haunting gaze of 1 million people, mostly children under five in Africa, who are dying of malaria from a mosquito bite. Here too our actions both simple and more involved will make a difference.

A Prescription for Change

We can't just hold our breath and hope it all goes away. The good news is that preventive care and timely treatment save lives and money. A full six-month course of TB treatment known as DOTS costs just $10 and spares lives by preventing the spread of the disease through coughing, sneezing, and even breathing. Educational campaigns, widespread testing, and access to treatment (including drugs that cost as little as $140 per year) can slow the spread and the devastation of HIV/AIDS. Malaria treatment costs just $2, and bed nets to prevent the mosquito bites that cause malaria cost only $5 each.

Governments, civil society, and individuals can do much more to remove the obstacles to care by addressing social unrest, management problems, inadequate health facility networks, and a shortage of trained health-care workers. Although there is no single cure-all, working together we can revive our commitment to health and wholeness for everyone. "The first wealth," wrote Ralph Waldo Emerson, "is health." When we invest in the health of our global community, we will all be the richer for it.

> ***"I believe that this could very well be looked back on as the sin of our generation. I look at my parents and ask, Where were they during the civil rights movement? I look at my grandparents and ask, What were they doing when the Holocaust in Europe was occurring with regard to the Jews, and why didn't they speak up? And when we think of our great, great, great-grandparents, we think, How could they have sat by and allowed slavery to exist? And I believe that our children and their children, forty or fifty years from now, are going to ask, What did you do while 40 million children became orphans in Africa?"***
>
> — Rich Stearns, president of World Vision

Imagine This...

What do you think has prevented people from acting to address health crises in our world? What do you believe will compel you to action? Envision what you would like to do and the difference you would like to make. If you are asked, ten years from now, what you did to help improve the health and save the lives of people around the world, what kind of answer will you give?

Healing a Hurting World

LEARN

☐ Watch the online films *Actions for Life* about the Global Plan to Stop TB at **<stoptb.org/globalplan>** and *Daring to Care* on the Global AIDS Alliance at **<globalaidsalliance.org>**.

☐ Explore the multimedia resources at the Roll Back Malaria Partnership **<rollbackmalaria.org>**.

☐ Visit the Web sites of the organizations mentioned in this chapter to learn more, join the mailing lists, and find out what you can do.

☐ Read *Mountains Beyond Mountains* by Tracy Kidder about the pioneering community health work of Dr. Paul Farmer and Partners in Health in Haiti. Recommend it to your book group or for discussion in your workplace, civic group, or place of worship. Visit **<pih.org>** for more information and opportunities to support the work of Partners in Health.

☐ Stay up-to-date with the Kaiser Network's Daily HIV/AIDS Report at **<kaisernetwork.org/daily_reports/rep_hiv.cfm>**.

☐ Learn more about people who are uninsured in the United States. Use the links at the Access Project Web site **<accessproject.org>** to connect to a wealth of organizations working on the crisis of the uninsured.

☐ Engage students in using the Lesson for Life materials on AIDS prepared by the Global Movement for Children **<gmfc.org>** and used by 15 million children and adults on World AIDS Day.

Jean, a Haitian teenager, was stunned when his mother told him that she and two of his three sisters were HIV-positive. "I won't lie to you," he said. "I didn't cry, but I was shocked. It took me two weeks to find the courage to tell my brother." A ray of hope came to the family from Arc-en-Ciel, an outreach program that helps children orphaned by AIDS-related illness or who have a parent living with HIV/AIDS. "Even though my mother is ill," Jean reports, "we are able to live the same way we always did." Arc-en-Ciel administers UNICEF-provided antiretroviral treatment that helps keep the parents alive and supports adults caring for orphaned children. The children receive good health care and monthly food rations for the family, and they are able to go to school, where they receive a hot meal as well as an education that less than one-third of Haitian children enjoy. The children are empowered to become part of the solution through conducting peer AIDS education in churches, schools, and community centers.

- ☐ Read "An African Miracle" by Christine Gorman in *Time* (November 2006) to learn more about what just a few doctors are doing to fight against AIDS **<time.com/time/magazine/article/0,9171,1562960,00.html>**.

- ☐ Read chapters 5 and 21 for more "I care about *your* health" information.

CONTRIBUTE

- ☐ Join the Change Me campaign, sponsored by Getty Images **<http://changeme.gettyimages.com>**. Select an image and tell the Friends of the Global Fight Against AIDS, Tuberculosis, and Malaria why the image motivates you, speaks to you, or inspires you to make a difference in the fight against these killer diseases. For every submission, Getty Images will donate $10 to the Friends of the Global Fight.

- ☐ Donate to pay for TB treatments and other work to stop TB by supporting the Call to Stop TB **<calltostoptb.org>**.

- ☐ Purchase (PRODUCT)red goods **<joinred.com>** to benefit the Global Fund to Fight AIDS, Tuberculosis, and Malaria **<theglobalfund.org>**.

- ☐ Collect medicine samples from your pharmacy and donate them to clinics serving low-income and uninsured patients.

- ☐ Contribute your professional medical skills and encourage your colleagues to do so as well. Opportunities are available through Partners in Health **<pih.org>**, the International Medical Volunteers Association **<imva.org>**, Health Volunteers Overseas **<hvousa.org>**, and the American Dental Association **<ada.org>**.

SERVE

- ☐ Sign on to join the Call to Stop TB **<calltostoptb.org>** and encourage others to do so.

- ☐ Arrange a showing and a discussion in your school, workplace, civic group, or place of worship of one or more of the following documentary films: *Hope to Fight For* (2004), narrated by Tom Hanks, about AIDS, TB, and malaria; *A Closer Walk* (2003), about AIDS; *Pandemic: Facing AIDS* (2003) by filmmaker Rory Kennedy, who puts a human face on a disease that's become a problem of global proportions; *Yesterday* (2005), the first Zulu-language film to be released internationally, about a woman who is HIV-positive and her family; and *Frontline: The Age of AIDS* (2006) by PBS Home Video.

- ☐ Involve your place of worship in the efforts of Religions for Peace **<wcrp.org>** and the Hope for African Children Initiative **<hopeforafricanchildren.org>** on behalf of children with HIV/AIDS. Religions for Peace will send you a CD-ROM with materials for your place of worship.

- ☐ Collaborate with friends to plan World TB Day or World AIDS Day events in your community to raise awareness and support for ending TB and AIDS. Or invite a health professional to address your school, workplace, civic group, or place of worship about these topics. Other good resources include the Student Global AIDS Campaign **<fightglobalaids.org>**, UNAIDS **<unaids.org>**, and Unite for Children, Unite Against AIDS **<unicef.org/uniteforchildren/index.html>**.

- ☐ Participate in or coordinate Cover the Uninsured Week events with your business, civic group, place of worship, or community to raise awareness of the 46.6 million Americans without health insurance. Visit **<covertheuninsured.org>** for fact sheets, planning resources, and information about scheduled events.

- ☐ Advocate for adequate resources for the Global Fund to Fight AIDS, Tuberculosis, and Malaria **<theglobalfund.org>** and other initiatives working to halt these diseases. For advocacy alerts and support, contact RESULTS **<results.org>**.

- ☐ Call for an urgent solution in the United States so that people can have the health-care coverage they need. Write letters to your elected representatives, conveying your concern about the problem of the uninsured and urging them to use their leadership to find solutions. Organizations such as Families USA **<familiesusa.org>** can provide information and support.

- ☐ Volunteer at a health clinic or for another health-related program locally or in a developing country and help provide medical care, support, supplies, or other assistance. You can explore opportunities online through the International Volunteer Programs Association **<volunteerinternational.org>** and Idealist **<idealist.org>**.

- ☐ Encourage your local hospital to increase the amount of charity care it provides.

- ☐ Find out who they are and support local dentists who provide pro bono work.

> *"If you focus on the enormity of the problem, you'll never get started."*
>
> — Dr. Mark Kline, pediatric AIDS specialist, Texas Children's Hospital

LIVE

- ☐ Get tested for TB and HIV/AIDS at appropriate intervals as recommended by your health-care provider and encourage others to do so as well.
- ☐ If you are a health professional, commit to donating care for one low-income patient for every twenty-five patients you serve.
- ☐ If you are an employer, provide good, affordable health-care coverage for your employees.

Actions Make a Difference

The U.S. Agency for International Development, the Canadian International Development Agency, and the government of the Netherlands came together in 2001 to create the Global Drug Facility, a key initiative of the Stop Tuberculosis Partnership, to make low-cost, high-quality lifesaving drugs available in donor-dependent countries as well as countries with sufficient finances that lack procurement or quality-assurance systems. As a result, more than 4 million TB patients in fifty-eight countries were treated in just four years.

CHAPTER 14

Provide Housing

There's no place like home. There's no place like home.

— Dorothy in
The Wizard of Oz

There's No Place Like Home

"Hey, I'm home!" Whether we're greeted by a loved one, a delighted pet, or even just a welcome and peaceful silence, there is nothing quite like coming home. For a family displaced by Hurricane Katrina moving into their new Habitat for Humanity home in Biloxi, or an impoverished family in Bangladesh using a microcredit loan to put a tin roof on their house to keep out the rain, or a refugee family getting settled in Boston, having the shelter of home is a wondrous experience.

Many, however, still have no place to call home. In the United States, 3.5 million people (including 1.3 million children) are homeless at some point every year. Millions more live in substandard housing that jeopardizes their health and safety, or they spend far too much of their income on housing and can't afford other necessities—like food.

Everyone deserves safe, decent, and affordable housing. UN Millennium Development Goal 7—ensure environmental sustainability—includes a target of significantly improving, by 2020, the lives of at least 100 million people in slums.

Around the world more than 1 billion people lack adequate housing and 100 million are homeless. These include refugees; people who are displaced within their own countries by war, drought, and disaster; those who live in slums; street children for whom

> *"Be conscientious about not viewing refugees as a faceless mass. Refugees are individuals. Each has a unique story of suffering and survival, unique hopes for happiness and security, unique strengths and skills and talents to offer to a new community."*
>
> — Lutheran Immigration and Refugee Service **<lirs.org>**

a highway overpass may be "home"; victims of forced evictions who are thrown out of their homes suddenly and often violently; and women without property rights who are thrust into homelessness and poverty by divorce, abandonment, or the death of a spouse.

Everyone needs and deserves a decent, safe, and affordable place to live, with water, sanitation, adequate living space, and protection from sudden, forced evictions. It will take more than a click of ruby slippers, but together we can work toward that day when everyone can come home.

Imagine This...

What if you couldn't go home tonight because someone there would harm you? What if you held the "wrong" religious beliefs and had to leave your community? What if you had to leave home only with what you could carry? What if you lived in a car? What if a natural disaster separated you from your family? Where would you go?

Opening Hearts, Minds, and Doors

LEARN

☐ Hear the stories of children who have lived on the street, profiled by Street Kids International **<streetkids.org>**. Discover ways you can support its efforts.

- ☐ Suggest to your group a book that deepens your understanding of homelessness, such as Jonathan Kozol's *Rachel and Her Children: Homeless Families in America.*

- ☐ Watch and discuss one or more of the following films about people without homes: *The Fisher King* (1991), about urban homelessness, starring Robin Williams; *Water* (2005), about a young Hindu widow; *Born into Brothels: Calcutta's Red Light Kids* (2004); and *Raja* or *Raja l'Africaine* (2003), about a 19-year-old Moroccan street orphan.

- ☐ Put a face on the homeless by inviting a speaker from the Faces of Homelessness Speakers' Bureau of the National Coalition for the Homeless to address your school, workplace, civic group, or place of worship. Find out how you can get involved in education, direct service, and advocacy efforts **<nationalhomeless.org>**.

- ☐ Arrange a screening, in your community or place of worship, of the one-hour documentary *Make Poverty Housing History* on affordable housing presented by the National Council of Churches **<ncccusa.org>**, featuring Christian, Jewish, and Muslim leaders, the president of Habitat for Humanity International, and others. Download the study guide at **<ncccusa.org/housing>** to use with your group.

- ☐ Find out more about the low-income rental market in your community. What kind of housing is available to people who are poor or have only a moderate income?

- ☐ Read chapter 22 to learn ways to improve access to clean water and sanitation—both crucial elements of adequate housing.

CONTRIBUTE

- ☐ Collect unused hotel toiletries when you travel and give them to a homeless shelter. Donate toys, books, clothing, and towels in good condition.

- ☐ Donate sheets, cribs, beds, pots and pans, and other household goods to a program helping people transition from homelessness into homes.

- ☐ Initiate at your place of worship a "housing emergency fund" that can be distributed in modest grants or interest-free loans to community members who need assistance paying utility bills or coming up with security deposits necessary to rent a home.

- ☐ Donate to organizations working to provide housing and related services for those in greatest need. For example, contributions to Street Kids International's "buy a chance for a better future" campaign provide resources to a targeted area, and you will be informed about their work, connected with youth workers and street kids in the region, and provided with regular updates **<streetkids.org>**.

- ☐ Respond to survivors made homeless by natural disasters. Contribute to efforts like the Ms. Foundation's Katrina Women's Response Fund **<ms.foundation.org>**, the Jericho Road Episcopal Housing Initiative in New Orleans **<er-d.org/katrina>**, and others rebuilding the Gulf Coast region. Keep in mind that most religious groups respond to disasters around the world as well as at home.

SERVE

- ☐ Support the work of an agency resettling refugees in the United States by assembling cleaning, hygiene, bedroom, or kitchen kits; donating household goods, furniture, or money; volunteering to provide transportation; welcoming adults and children and introducing them to the community and its resources; or providing other needed help. Search *refugee resettlement agencies* online to find a group.

- ☐ Work with your place of worship to co-sponsor a refugee through a resettlement agency. This commitment typically covers the individual's first few months, assisting with rent, food, clothing, and other material needs as well as providing friendship, transportation, and other support.

- ☐ Volunteer with Habitat for Humanity **<habitat.org>**, a nonprofit, nondenominational Christian organization that partners with those who need shelter to build simple, affordable houses; you can help on or off the construction site in the United States or around the world.

- ☐ Travel to serve with Bridges to Community **<bridgestocommunity.org>**, a community development group that organizes volunteers to learn, serve, and reflect as they participate in construction, health, and education projects in developing countries.

- ☐ Organize volunteers through your school, workplace, civic group, or place of worship to help repair the homes of elderly or low-income people or teach home-repair skills. Work with a social service organization to identify families in need.

☐ Volunteer at a homeless shelter. Organize recreation and tutoring for children. Help adults gain job search skills.

> *"They forgot we were there."*
>
> — A nine-year-old as he tried to explain the long wait for a meal and shelter he endured with his grandmother and three siblings at a New York City homeless intake center

☐ Advocate for federal, state, and local housing policies that increase the supply of safe and affordable housing, promote inclusionary zoning, and provide safety nets for those who are homeless or living in "worst-case" housing. Organizations such as the National Low Income Housing Coalition **<nlihc.org>** can provide information and support in speaking out for good housing.

☐ Support your local community development corporation's efforts to build affordable housing.

☐ Volunteer with a local community agency to help people learn about basic banking services and combat predatory lending practices. Visit ACORN **<acorn.org>** to learn more about its community organizing work to improve housing and eliminate predatory lending.

☐ Encourage people you know with legal skills to lend them to local legal clinics and housing coalitions.

☐ Urge your employer to participate in state or local home ownership or asset-building programs.

LIVE

- ☐ Build a greater sense of community in your neighborhood. Start a block organization to help neighbors support one another, whether its keeping an eye on children and house-bound seniors, helping with property cleanup, creating a community garden, or supporting victims of domestic abuse.
- ☐ Purchase housing affordable to subsequent owners by buying into a limited equity housing cooperative (LEHC) or a land trust. To learn more about LEHCs, see **<policylink.org/EDTK/LEHC>**.
- ☐ Maximize the use of your own property. If you have a large, underutilized house or apartment, seek roommates or establish an accessory dwelling unit. If you have a large lot, build an additional, affordable unit.
- ☐ Wear a button that says *YIMBY* ("Yes, in my backyard!").

Students of St. James School in Hagerstown, Maryland, selected the Da Nang Street Children's Program of the Global Community Service Foundation **<globalcommunityservice.org>** for their community service day during a two-week educational program in Viet Nam. The students raised several thousand dollars to sponsor two new houses for families living at the Da Nang garbage dump, purchased an industrial sewing machine for vocational training, donated twenty bikes for boys living in one of the Da Nang Street Kids houses, and hosted a dinner for some of the street children.

- ☐ Consider choosing to live in more densely settled communities with set-aside green space to combat sprawl.

Actions Make a Difference

For Dorothy Howard's family in Houston, Texas, and Santa Cruz Parades's family in Bolivia, opening the door to their new homes built with support from Habitat for Humanity brought them across the threshold to a hopeful future. They joined the more than two hundred thousand families living in houses built in partnership with Habitat for Humanity around the world. Thanks to Habitat for Humanity and the families and community volunteers who have taken hammer in hand to tackle the housing crisis head-on, more than 1 million people in more than three thousand communities now have safe, decent, affordable shelter. That's some homecoming!

CHAPTER 15

Call for Debt Relief

People from the world's richest countries should be prepared to accept the burden of debt reduction for heavily indebted poor countries and should urge their leaders to fulfill the pledges made to reduce world poverty, especially in Africa, by the year 2015.

— Pope Benedict XVI, message to the Make Poverty History March, July 2, 2005

Forgive Us Our Debts...

Debt. Most of us have it. Some of it is "smart" debt—a mortgage that is slowly but surely securing a home for our family or a college loan that enabled an education that prepared us for a good job. Some is not-so-smart debt—the kind we bring on ourselves, with high credit card interest rates, to pay for luxuries we could have done without. And then there are the painful mountains of debt, like medical bills we couldn't avoid and can't afford or debt incurred by an irresponsible family member, with which we are now saddled. How much debt we have, and what kind, has a significant impact on our well-being and affects how we live.

Like each of us, the world's poorest countries are saddled with various kinds of debt—repaying rich countries and international institutions such as the World Bank and the International Monetary Fund (IMF) for a variety of loans. Some of this borrowed money went to prop up military regimes that are now long gone. Some of it was spent unwisely. Some came from rich countries to

A key component of UN Millennium Development Goal 8—develop a global partnership for development—is debt relief.

serve their own self-interests. Some debts accumulated in the aftermath of natural disasters. Despite the fact that African countries have paid back $10 billion *more* than the amount of loans received between 1970 and 2002, the skyrocketing interest rates of the late 1970s and the early 1980s mean they still owe nearly $300 billion. The debt burden means that many poor countries spend far more paying off interest than on schools, hospitals, and other investments that would reduce poverty and strengthen incomes and futures.

...As We Forgive Our Debtors

Finally, beginning in 1999, rich countries responded to public calls for "Jubilee" debt relief and have begun writing off much of poor countries' debt through the World Bank and the IMF's Enhanced Heavily Indebted Poor Countries program. It's not a "get out of debtors jail free" card, however. The forty countries (all but six are in Africa) in the program must have strong governments that commit to fight corruption and poverty and invest in education and health care.

What's *Jubilee*? In the Bible, Leviticus 25, Moses was instructed by God to make every fiftieth year a Jubilee year. Debts were forgiven, property and land lost because of debt was restored, and communities torn apart by inequality were healed. Jubilee USA Network **<jubileeusa.org>** is an alliance of seventy-five religious denominations and faith communities together with labor, community, human rights, and environmental groups—all working for the definitive cancellation of crushing debts to fight poverty and injustice in Asia, Africa, and Latin America. The Jubilee Congregations program grew from discussions within a regional Jubilee group about strategies to involve local churches at the grassroots level. Out of the seeds of this vision, Jubilee Congregations has grown from a church-based effort to an interfaith dialogue and a national network. Your group can join. A little goes a long way.

The remaining debt, however, has continued to debilitate these countries' efforts to get back on track, and the financial institutions are now moving to forgive not just a portion but *all* of the old debt and in the future to give money as grants rather than loans. Debt relief isn't the only answer to solving the problems in developing countries, but wiping the slate clean of decades-old debt is giving many a fresh start to invest in education, health care, and economic progress.

Imagine This…

Imagine that your grandfather borrowed hundreds of thousands of dollars. He didn't pay it off before he died, and now you must. As a result, you can't buy a house; you can't even take your children to the doctor or pay for school tuition or supplies. Furthermore, you can't declare bankruptcy. So you have to borrow more money just to pay off your existing debts, digging yourself into a still deeper hole. Imagine knowing that your own children will inherit this massive debt. How will they pay it back without the benefit of a good education and job prospects?

Now imagine that entire debt has just been forgiven.

Relieving the Burden of Debt

LEARN

- ☐ Visit the Web site for DATA (Debt, AIDS, Trade, Africa) **<data.org>** and learn how we can respond to the crises swamping Africa: unpayable debts, the uncontrolled spread of AIDS, and unfair trade rules that keep Africans poor.

- ☐ Read "A Beginner's Guide to the Debt Crisis" at **<jubileeusa.org>** (click on "Learn more" on the home page).

☐ Gather a group of friends, colleagues, or members of your religious or civic group and watch films about debt relief. Options include *Hope in Hard Times* (2004), a documentary recording the responses of ordinary people to Argentina's 2002 economic crash, and *Life and Debt* (2001), about Jamaica, caught in the web of international systems.

☐ Organize a simple meal at your workplace or place of worship and provide information or a short video on how unfair indebtedness causes malnutrition. Arrange to set up an informational display for others to see.

☐ Talk to a teacher to see if you might present an age-appropriate exercise on debt issues to a class. Depending on the class's area of study, you can relate it to math, economics, social science, geography, or history.

☐ Discover what resources your religious tradition has to support your advocacy of debt relief. Many national offices of religious bodies, including the U.S. Conference of Catholic Bishops **<usccb.org/sdwp/globalpoverty>**, the Religious Action Center of Reform Judaism **<rac.org>**, and a variety of Protestant denominations, are working for debt relief and post resources on their Web sites.

☐ Listen to *Break the Chains!,* a musical CD available from **<jubileeusa.org>**.

CONTRIBUTE

☐ Donate to organizations working for debt relief, such as DATA and Jubilee USA.

- ☐ Recognize the value of your voice in calling for debt relief: "contribute" letters, e-mails, and phone calls to decision-makers.

SERVE

- ☐ Work with your place of worship to become a Jubilee Congregation that contributes $1 and one letter per member to advocate for debt relief and may make additional commitments to study and act.
- ☐ Speak out for debt relief by communicating with your elected officials and the media. For support and resources, connect with DATA, Jubilee USA, and other organizations working for the cause.
- ☐ Write a short commentary for a local paper on debt relief for heavily indebted poor countries.
- ☐ Gather a small group and make appointments to meet with your congressional representatives to explain your concerns about debt policies and developing countries.

LIVE

- ☐ Create a financial plan for yourself that eliminates unnecessary debt, frees you from being financially overextended, and enables you to contribute to organizations fighting for more-just debt refinancing.
- ☐ Work to elect public officials who understand global poverty issues and are dedicated to eliminating poverty in our lifetimes—or become one of those candidates!

Actions Make a Difference

Debt relief, reports DATA, enabled Uganda to double primary school enrollment, invest in a national HIV/AIDS plan that reversed infection rates, and build clean water wells. It enabled Mozambique to immunize a half million children and build and electrify schools, and it enabled Tanzania to invest in education and eliminate grade school fees so an estimated 1.6 million children could return to school. Thanks to debt relief, Benin could eliminate school fees in rural areas.

CHAPTER 16

Serve with Satisfaction

More Thoughts on Volunteering

I would like to do whatever it is that
presses the essence from the hour.

— Mary Oliver, American poet

Time to Act

Have you ever thought about the phrase *spending time*? Our time is valuable, and we never get a spent minute back. Because time is precious, we don't want to waste it. Chances are, if you are holding this book in your hands, you believe that helping others is one of the most worthwhile ways you can spend your time.

Even so, volunteering isn't a one-size-fits-all proposition. We have to make thoughtful decisions about how to spend our valuable time. Questions to ask yourself might include: *What can I do that will ignite my passion, commitment, and creativity? What are my greatest gifts and interests, and how can I use them to make a difference? What skills and experience could I draw on? What aspects of poverty and the UN Millennium Development Goals do I find most compelling or am I most drawn to help solve? Do I want to get involved by myself, or do I want to find an opportunity to serve with my family, friends, colleagues, or others? What kind of time commitments will work best with my schedule? What commitments can I sustain?*

There are lots of ways to find the opportunities and the organizations that match your interests, skills, experience, time, and concerns as you work to end poverty in our day. This book offers you hundreds of ideas for what you can do and whom you can contact to get started. But they are just the tip of the iceberg. Using the Internet, you can connect with any of a number of volunteer-matching sites that ask you to submit information (such as your ZIP code) and your areas of interest (such as poverty or health care) and then produce a range of opportunities.

Other service-oriented Web sites and blogs don't match you with actual organizations but rather list key actions that you can take by connecting with an appropriate organization in your community. Other volunteer organizations focus on particular groups of people, such as students, retirees, singles, twenty-somethings, families, or religious, racial, ethnic, or alumni connections.

> ***"The things to do are the things that need doing, that you see need to be done, and that no one else seems to see need to be done."***
>
> — Buckminster Fuller, American philosopher, architect, and inventor

There is the possibility that the perfect volunteer opportunity doesn't yet exist except in your imagination. But you can always create it! If you have an idea of how you want to share your time, doing something that you love to do, that you think will make a positive difference to a situation you care about, that will contribute to the end of poverty in our day—by all means suggest it to someone who is working with or on behalf of those you want to serve.

Elements of Community Service

Campus Outreach Opportunity League (COOL) has identified "Five Critical Elements of Community Service." As you explore volunteer opportunities, see if the program or organization has these elements in place.

1. **Community voice.** The community to be served has a voice in the development of the planned service.
2. **Orientation and training.** Volunteers are prepared to serve appropriately and effectively.
3. **Meaningful action.** The service provided is necessary and valuable to those served, and volunteers feel well utilized.
4. **Reflection.** Volunteers have an opportunity to reflect on and share their service experience and place it in a broader context.
5. **Evaluation.** The organization assesses the impact of the service on the volunteer and on those served. Both volunteers and those served should have an opportunity to evaluate.

No Time Like the Present

Volunteer service opportunities are suggested throughout this book. Begin to think more broadly about the kinds of service activities that will be most satisfying to you. If possible, commit to doing them more than once. Consistency of service is greatly valued. Whether it's driving meals to people, escorting folks to the doctor, or helping them with their income tax and financial planning, you will find that the friendship will become as important as the actual deed itself.

Imagine This...

What skills or activities bring you the deepest satisfaction? How could you use that experience to ease suffering, enrich impoverished lives, help those disenfranchised to claim their power and voice, and help bring about the end of poverty?

Reflecting on Your Gifts for and Interest in Service

- ☐ Make two lists: the things you love to do most and the problems that you most want to help solve to contribute to the end of poverty in our day. Think creatively and expansively about how you might connect them in a volunteer commitment that could make a positive difference.

- ☐ Assess your most enduring commitments. What have you done that sustained your commitment for the longest time? What kept you committed? Now think about commitments that you broke or that you couldn't wait to be over. Why did your commitment wane? Apply those insights as you make a new volunteer commitment.

- ☐ Evaluate your current schedule realistically. What new time commitments would work best for you? A fixed weekly commitment of just an hour? A half-day commitment once a month? A flexible commitment that can adapt to a travel schedule? Something that can be done in brief increments at home? A several-week service trip once a year?

- ☐ Think about how to best engage others. Would you enjoy and sustain your volunteer commitment more if you were doing it with others, such as friends, family, colleagues, neighbors, or members of your congregation or civic group? The more people involved, the bigger difference you will make.

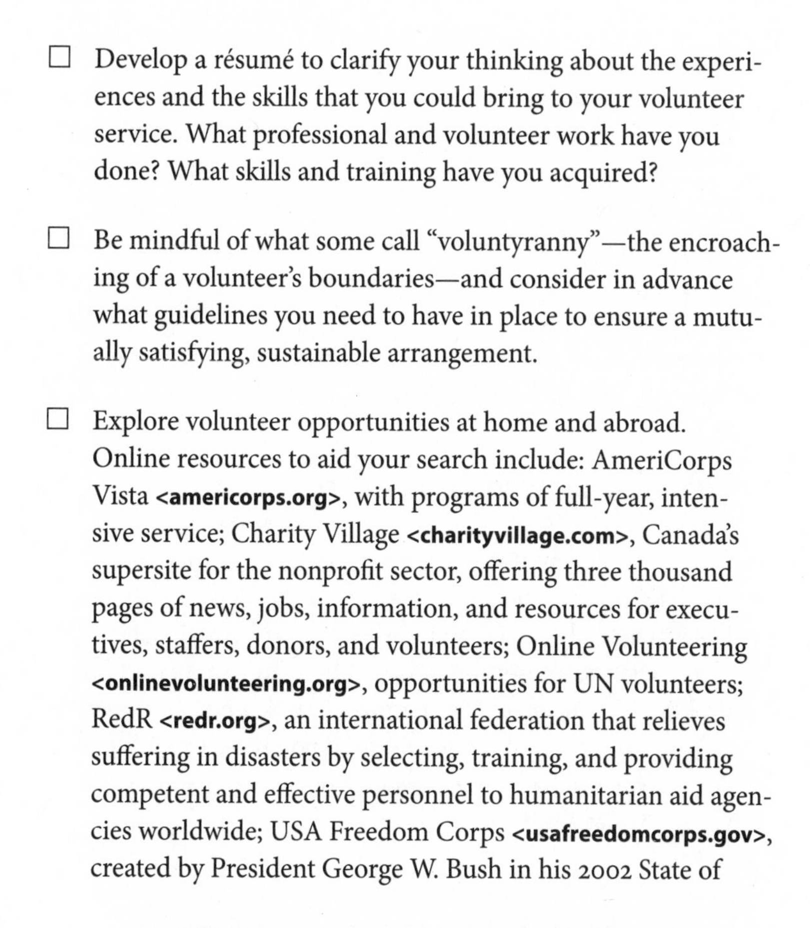

☐ Develop a résumé to clarify your thinking about the experiences and the skills that you could bring to your volunteer service. What professional and volunteer work have you done? What skills and training have you acquired?

☐ Be mindful of what some call "voluntyranny"—the encroaching of a volunteer's boundaries—and consider in advance what guidelines you need to have in place to ensure a mutually satisfying, sustainable arrangement.

☐ Explore volunteer opportunities at home and abroad. Online resources to aid your search include: AmeriCorps Vista **<americorps.org>**, with programs of full-year, intensive service; Charity Village **<charityvillage.com>**, Canada's supersite for the nonprofit sector, offering three thousand pages of news, jobs, information, and resources for executives, staffers, donors, and volunteers; Online Volunteering **<onlinevolunteering.org>**, opportunities for UN volunteers; RedR **<redr.org>**, an international federation that relieves suffering in disasters by selecting, training, and providing competent and effective personnel to humanitarian aid agencies worldwide; USA Freedom Corps **<usafreedomcorps.gov>**, created by President George W. Bush in his 2002 State of

> *"I am of the opinion that my life belongs to the whole community,…and it is my privilege to do for it whatever I can. I want to be thoroughly used up when I die, for the harder I work, the more I live. I rejoice in life for its own sake. Life is no brief candle to me. It is a sort of splendid torch which I've got a hold of for the moment, and I want to make it burn as brightly as possible before handing it on to the future generations."*
>
> — George Bernard Shaw, *Man and Superman*

the Union Address to strengthen and expand the volunteer service, sacrifice, and generosity that followed September 11; Volunteer Match **<volunteermatch.org>**, a U.S.-based volunteer clearinghouse; and World Volunteer Web **<worldvolunteerweb.org>**, a global clearinghouse for information and resources linked to volunteerism that can be used for campaigning, advocacy, and networking in support of the UN Millennium Development Goals; it is part of the United Nations Volunteers program and partners with more than twenty thousand organizations and individuals.

Engaging in Service with Others

☐ Involve members of your ongoing group in periodic service activities that will help end poverty and related problems. For instance, if you have a book group, one month collect new books for a resource-poor public school or a Head Start program. If you have a dinner group, cook a meal for several refugee families a few times a year. If you have a standing Saturday basketball game, organize occasional games with youngsters at a homeless shelter.

☐ Join in a day of service, such as Make a Difference Day **<usaweekend.com/diffday>**, sponsored by *USA Weekend*, Newman's Own, and the Points of Light Foundation; Martin Luther King Jr. Day of Service **<mlkday.gov>**; Join Hands Day **<joinhandsday.org>**, sponsored by America's Fraternal Benefit Societies; and National and Global Youth Service Day **<ysa.org>**, sponsored by Youth Service America. Many local communities and organizations also sponsor service days. Your one day of service may spark a connection to a new, ongoing service need or opportunity.

When young social worker Jamilla Larsen learned that children as young as three to thirteen were being placed in a cavernous homeless shelter for adults, she felt heartsick but not hopeless. She sprung into action. Within weeks she had organized recreation and tutoring for the children in the shelter, soliciting donations of toys and books from the community and recruiting volunteers from nearby offices that agreed to give employees time off to volunteer. She also got involved in trying to change policies that led to such an inappropriate placement, meeting with the mayor and becoming an outspoken advocate for the children. The children are now placed in a family shelter, where Jamilla continues to organize volunteers for weekly activities through her Homeless Children's Playtime Project **<playtimeproject.org>**. It didn't take a lot of money or expertise, just love, determination, and a vision that captured others' desire to help.

- ☐ If you are a college student or live in a college town, check out the campus's service organizations, clubs, and opportunities, or work to start a group that will contribute to meeting the UN Millennium Development Goals.

- ☐ Contact organizations that offer opportunities for people with your particular level of expertise and which can help you bring your skills, experience, and time to help others move out of poverty. If you are retired, consider the Retired Volunteer Service Corps **<seniorcorps.org>**. If you are over fifty-five, contact Experience Corps **<experiencecorps.org>**. The Peace Corps needs experienced adults, too **<peacecorps.gov>**.

- ☐ If you are employed, find out about corporate volunteerism programs or if your employer would release you for a certain amount of time to volunteer with a program working to end poverty. Many companies support and promote employee volunteering because of its benefits to communities, employees, and the companies themselves. Building Blocks International **<bblocks.org>**, for instance, helps develop corporate programs.

☐ If you have children at home, hold a family meeting to discuss what your family could do to help others. Select a project or two that will engage your children in addressing poverty. Even young children, for instance, could help put cans in grocery bags at a community food pantry.

☐ With your child, visit Do Something at **<dosomething.org>**. It offers an online community for young people, where they can learn, listen, speak, vote, volunteer, ask, and take action to make the world a better place.

Supporting Service Learning

☐ Support service-learning requirements in schools, whereby students are required to fulfill a certain number of hours of community service. Learn more at National Service-Learning Clearinghouse, **<servicelearning.org>**.

☐ If you're involved with a program that is meeting the needs of people who are poor, explore how you might become a service-learning site for students in the community so that they might become better informed about the problems of poverty and ways to address them.

Expanding the Scope of Your Service Commitment

- ☐ Check out Action Without Borders **<idealist.org>**, a global clearinghouse of nonprofit and volunteering resources that includes a directory of fifty-nine thousand nonprofits and community organizations in 165 countries. It offers tools for nonprofits and lists volunteer opportunities, job information, and salary surveys.

- ☐ Explore service programs that make use of your professional skills (such as medicine, construction, accounting, writing, or teaching) to contribute to reaching the UN Millennium Development Goals.

- ☐ Explore whether a yearlong or multiyear commitment to a domestic or international service program working to end poverty is right for you. Most programs welcome volunteers from every stage of life, from recent graduates to retirees.

- ☐ Consider a new career that addresses the causes and effects of poverty, such as teaching in underprivileged schools through Teach For America **<teachforamerica.org>**.

- ☐ Extend your impact. Don't let your contribution end with your hands-on service. Seek opportunities to talk to others about your service work and how they too can make a difference. Offer to give a talk or lead a class at your school, workplace, civic group, or place of worship. Write articles about your work for newsletters and other publications. Send an e-mail to your contact list to inspire others to take action. Use your firsthand experience to advocate for systemic change to help prevent problems and to expand effective solutions.

Actions Make a Difference

Richard Berger, like many of us, was overwhelmed by the news of the 2005 earthquake in Pakistan that left 3 million people facing a frigid winter without shelter. "The problem was so large, I couldn't get my head around it," he confessed in an article in the *Seattle Times* (December 25, 2005). So his first response was to ignore it. But then he began to reduce the mind-boggling disaster to more-manageable questions: *What difference could a tent or even a hiker's survival blanket make to ward off deadly hypothermia? What could one person do?* Berger purchased several types of survival blankets from a nearby REI store, tested them to find the best, and then called the manufacturer, who agreed to drop the cost from $5.50 to just $1. Berger's next call was to the relief agency Mercy Corps, which agreed to distribute the blankets. An e-mail to 250 friends brought in donations, and then the delivery company DHL got word of his efforts and offered to ship some for free. What can one person do? Berger answered his own question with astonishing success: more than 110,000 thermal blankets were sent to Pakistan as the result of his actions.

PART III

Evening

CHAPTER 17

Extend Hospitality and Create Community

I'm gonna sit at the welcome table
one of these days, hallelujah.

I'm gonna tell God how you treat me
one of these days, hallelujah.

All God's children gonna sit together
one of these days, hallelujah.

— African-American spiritual

A Place at the Table

What makes you feel truly welcome? Can you recall a time when you left someone's home after dinner, aglow with the hospitality you received? What happened during that time that made you feel so welcome?

Dinner isn't always, or even often, an experience that epitomizes that fullest sense of hospitality. Instead it may be a solitary affair or squeezed between family members' many commitments. Dinner is often consumed in transit or rushed onto the table; it might be eaten in silence or drowned out by the TV.

Perhaps because experiences of true hospitality are more elusive, they are all the more precious when they happen. Meals can do so much more than nourish our bodies. When we create a warm and true spirit of hospitality, dinner is a time of conversation, a way of forging community and deepening relationship, a chance to share concerns, questions, hopes, and dreams. It is a time to reflect on our day and to look ahead to tomorrow.

Hospitality creates relationships needed to understand and tackle the intricacies of poverty so that we can eradicate extreme hunger and poverty and meet Millennium Development Goal 1.

Just as our bodies hunger for nourishment, our hearts and minds yearn to make a difference with our lives and to experience community. How can dinner become an occasion of meaningful hospitality and an opportunity to nourish commitment to ending poverty? Whom might you invite to join you? What might you talk about? What if you raised some of the actions you've been reading about in this book? What could you do together? How can you create inclusive community through the hospitality that you extend in all areas of your life?

Imagine This…

If the world were represented by just ten people and you invited them for dinner…

- Two of your guests would earn less than $1 per day.
- Two would speak a Chinese dialect.
- Two couldn't read or write.
- Three wouldn't have access to clean water.
- Four wouldn't have access to improved sanitation.
- Four would be under nineteen years old.
- Five would be malnourished.

(Some guests are represented in more than one category.)

Making Sure Everyone Has a Place at the Table

LEARN

- ☐ See chapters 1 and 9 to learn more about hunger, malnutrition, and starvation; read chapter 6 to think more deeply about agriculture and global food production. Share what you learn with your friends.

- ☐ With children you know, share the book *If the World Were a Village: A Book About the World's People* by David J. Smith and talk about what it means to be part of the global community and how we can be hospitable to our worldwide family.

- ☐ Watch *Babette's Feast* (1988) with your friends and talk about service, scarcity, and abundance in your own community.

- ☐ Work with your schools and workplace to develop antiracism education and training and to encourage multicultural education. The Anti-Defamation League's World of Difference **<adl.org>** program has resources for all ages and many settings.

- ☐ Use the menu to get conversation going; menus can be history, math, science, and social studies rolled into one. How might we use Thanksgiving, Passover, Ramadan, and Cinco de Mayo to frame dialogue about building community and ending poverty in our world?

- ☐ Learn another language. It will increase your ability to develop friendships, understand other communities, and be of service.

☐ Keep a map or globe handy in your home. When you hear news about an unfamiliar country, locate it. Talk about how this relates to you.

☐ Check out United Planet **<unitedplanet.org>**, an international nonprofit fostering cross-cultural understanding and friendship through educational, humanitarian, and peace-building initiatives.

CONTRIBUTE

☐ Host a fund-raiser. Have a small group over for a meal with the invitation to make a contribution to your favorite nonprofit organization helping to end hunger and poverty. Some organizations offer materials and tips; others leave it up to you.

☐ Participate in Wine.Dine.Donate, a partnership between America's Second Harvest **<secondharvest.org>** and Epicurious **<epicurious.com>**, to raise funds for the domestic

Bill Drayton, founder of Ashoka Foundation, which supports social entrepreneurs, frequently hosts dinners. Unlike the typical Washington party circuit, these dinners aren't about the menu, although the food is usually delicious, or the "scene," although guests are often those whom others would love to meet. Instead Bill gathers people to a meal to talk about a big idea or topic or the transformative work each is engaged in to protect the environment, reduce poverty, spread microcredit, or some other effort. He puts careful thought into inviting those whom he thinks will have an insight or a perspective or an experience to bring to the table. When guests leave one of Bill's dinners, they are filled not just with good food but with new ideas and possibilities brimming in their hearts and minds. They have been fed.

hunger programs that feed almost seventy thousand hungry people every day. Prepare the monthly menus suggested by famous chefs, invite friends to dine and pay a suggested $50 contribution to America's Second Harvest, or attend one of the dinners at a participating restaurant.

SERVE

- ☐ Host a dinner—as casual or as fancy as you like—and invite guests to talk about the UN Millennium Development Goals and what we can do together about the world's most dire poverty. Distribute this book or fact sheets and other materials from **<millenniumpromise.org>**.

- ☐ Serve up support. Volunteer at a community kitchen or food pantry and look for ways to express hospitality, whether serving food, playing with children, sitting down with guests, or making the site more inviting.

- ☐ Set an extra place. Contact an immigrant and refugee resettlement organization and arrange to invite a recently arrived individual or family to share a meal with you. Many do this during the holiday season, but how about extending it to ordinary mealtimes?

- ☐ Spread cheer. If your place of worship or a community agency delivers holiday meals to local families, look into providing meals at other times throughout the year, too. Cook the meals with friends or family members and then deliver them to people in your community who would welcome them.

- ☐ Open hearts and doors. Plan a Thanksgiving dinner at your place of worship or other community setting. Open it to all regardless of the ability to pay or contribute dishes. Contact restaurants and stores for contributions.
- ☐ Develop a vision and plan to encourage an inclusive, intergenerational response to hunger so that children, senior citizens, and everyone in between could have their nutritional needs met in a joyful, safe, nurturing, and lively community setting.

LIVE

- ☐ Just talk. Have dinner with your friends and family—together—on a regular basis and talk about the world. Make the connections with loved ones or in personal reflection.
- ☐ Speak up when you hear someone perpetuating a stereotype. Racism, sexism, and other biases against people of other nationalities, languages, and incomes create and perpetuate poverty and injustice.
- ☐ Seek out opportunities to join or create inclusive communities, from where you live to where you worship, learn, work, and spend recreational time.
- ☐ Open your home to a student participating in an intercultural exchange program such as AFS **<afs.org>**.
- ☐ Give thanks at mealtime, remembering your global family.

Actions Make a Difference

Robert Egger sees potential everywhere—in people some would cast aside and in food others would throw away. The D.C. Central Kitchen (DCCK) **<dccentralkitchen.org>** he founded began operations redistributing excess food from the 1989 presidential inauguration. Every day, the DCCK recycles more than a ton of surplus food from local food service establishments and turns it into four thousand meals for people who are hungry. The skilled hands preparing the food are participants in DCCK's rigorous Culinary Job Training Program. Once homeless and hungry themselves, these cooks are now feeding others while gaining professional and life skills for employment in the food service industry.

Egger doesn't like the term *soup kitchen,* which conjures up old stereotypes of who is hungry. He prefers *community kitchen.* Egger's capacity to create community is heard in the words of Michael Sims, one of his trainees who worked hard to overcome addiction, incarceration, and other challenges to successfully graduate from the training program. "All my life I haven't really fit in," Sims told the *Washington Post.* "At the kitchen I started to feel like I belonged, that the people around had my back."

CHAPTER 18

Spread Literacy

Once you learn to read, you will be forever free.

— Frederick Douglass, American journalist and abolitionist

Once Upon a Time

Do you love settling in with a good book before going to sleep, or perhaps snuggling a child next to you and reading a bedtime story? Do you remember as a child reading a book that opened up a new world to you, or have you read a book more recently that gave you a new perspective? Books like the one you're holding in your hand right now can open doors to a better future and create opportunities to make a difference.

Three-quarters of a billion adults worldwide (that's one in five) can't read the words on this page. In the United States alone, 42 million adults cannot read. Illiteracy not only excludes them from the rich and lively world of books but can have a detrimental impact on their income and well-being, preventing them from getting or keeping jobs, signing up for public benefits for which they are eligible, reading about services that could assist them, and providing for themselves and their families.

Literacy is a key to work, education, and other opportunities. UN Millennium Development Goal 3 calls on us to promote gender equality and empower women, eliminating gender disparity at all levels of education by no later than 2015.

My husband didn't want me to send my five children to school because his parents didn't send him to school. From the beginning he said he would not pay, and he has never given even one *goud,* but I always knew it was important. For a long time, I have gone to Port-au-Prince to buy goods to sell in Hinche, and I put all my money into paying for school for my children.

When I found out that Fonkoze [a microcredit program in Haiti] gave literacy classes for market women, I was so happy. I never went to school even one day. I didn't know anything about school. I started right away with basic literacy, and I have tried to never miss a class. I couldn't write my name, and I didn't understand anything, but I kept going even when my husband got angry. My kids pushed me and encouraged me and they helped me practice my letters.... I can write my name now, and I write it everywhere.

I used to go to Port-au-Prince to buy [products for my microbusiness], and I couldn't read the bags and I felt lost. I couldn't keep track of what I bought. The drivers sometimes would take my boxes off the truck and give them to someone else, but I didn't know until I got all the way home. Now I can't lose anything; now I write my name on every box and I know what I buy.

— Janèt Dèval, Haiti

And They All Lived Happily Ever After

The challenges people like Janèt Dèval face are multiplied millions of times around the world. So too are the opportunities to make a difference. Ending illiteracy is one of the easiest challenges our world faces: we know what the problem is and its causes and, most important, the solution is one to which virtually every one of us who can read can contribute. In some instances creating literacy requires money, but often it simply requires our time and willingness to help.

Imagine This...

Pick up a copy of an important form (such as tax preparation forms at the post office) in a language you cannot read. Try to fill it out. What if, every day, you were unable to read important information? What impact would it have on your employment, income, and well-being?

Helping Others Start a New Chapter in Their Lives

LEARN

☐ Visit the National Institute for Literacy **<nifl.gov>** or ProLiteracy Worldwide **<proliteracy.org>** to learn more about who reads and who can't and how we can help.

☐ Read and discuss with others books about poverty such as those recommended throughout these chapters.

☐ Learn more about teaching English as a second language **<esl.com>**. For ESL resources go to **<owl.english.purdue.edu/handouts/esl>**.

CONTRIBUTE

☐ Support organizations providing new or used books to people who need them, including the International Book Project **<intlbookproject.org>**, First Book **<firstbook.org>**, and Room to Read **<roomtoread.org>**. You can donate used books, give money to cover shipping a mailbag full of books, or underwrite the cost of creating a library room, school room, or computer room in another country.

- ☐ Dig out those no-longer-used eyeglasses, reading glasses, and sunglasses and bring them to an AAA service center, a LensCrafters store, or to a local Lions Club. Your donation will help others see.

- ☐ Sell your used books online and give the profits to a library or literacy program; **<ebay.com>**, **<amazon.com>**, and **<half.com>** are likely places.

- ☐ Donate used books to programs serving low-income children or adults.

- ☐ Click and give books at no cost to you. There's a big red button at **<firstbook.org>**. By partnering with site sponsors and First Book, more than 40 million books have already reached children in hundreds of communities.

- ☐ Involve children in your class or neighborhood in a read-a-thon, collecting pledges for each page read during a certain period of time. (For instance, someone might pledge $0.10 for every page a child reads during the designated week.) Donate all of the money collected to a domestic or international literacy program, or purchase books to donate to a resource-poor school or reading program.

> ***"My mother read poetry to me before I could read, and I can't remember when I couldn't read. We grew up with books. I don't think you can write if you don't read. You can't read if you can't think. Thinking, reading, and writing all go together. When I was about eight, I decided that the most wonderful thing, next to a human being, was a book."***
>
> — Dr. Margaret Walker Alexander, U.S. author and poet, in Brian Lanker's *I Dream a World: Portraits of Black Women Who Changed America*

- ☐ Support the development and the replication of self-led literacy programs like the Empowerment Program **<empowermentprogram.org>**. Through its Pact program **<pactworld.org>**, groups train their own teachers and raise funds for their books and the lamps by which they study. You can support them by making donations to the Empowerment Program or by forming an Empowerment Circle, a group that sets fund-raising targets and reaches out to friends and networks to donate time, funds, and connections.

SERVE

- ☐ Volunteer with an adult literacy program once a week. Many provide simple training sessions for their volunteers. Find an organization near you at **<literacydirectory.org>**.
- ☐ Travel to another country and volunteer with a literacy program. See chapter 20 for suggestions on finding a suitable opportunity.
- ☐ Read to children in Head Start programs, child-care programs serving low-income children, health clinic waiting rooms, public schools, juvenile detention facilities, or another location in your community.
- ☐ Help reach out to and enroll people who are eligible for public programs (like the Earned Income Tax Credit program or the State Children's Health Insurance Program) but are not enrolled, often because their lack of reading skills prevents them from learning about or signing up for the benefits. The Center on Budget and Policy Priorities, the Children's Defense Fund, Covering Kids & Families, and other nonprofit organizations have materials to help get you started.

LIVE

- ☐ Read to your children or grandchildren every day and let people see you reading for enjoyment. If the children are older, take turns reading aloud to each other from a book the whole family enjoys.

Actions Make a Difference

In the United States, adult reading scores improve approximately one grade level with just thirty-five to forty hours of tutoring.

CHAPTER 19

Improve Transportation Options

All I was doing was trying to get home from work.

— Rosa Parks, American civil rights leader

How Do You Fare?

From Boston to Beijing, Denver to Dhaka, Soweto to San Francisco, people are on the move. Most of us drive, walk, cycle, or take a bus or train to and from work. When we can't get where we need to go reliably, efficiently, and economically, it can have a huge impact on our income and well-being. Those of us with low incomes often face tremendous obstacles. We may not be able to afford a car, gas, insurance, repairs, parking, and other costs. We may not live near public transportation. Perhaps we can't afford it or we find it unreliable and time-consuming, especially if we have to take a child to school or child care before getting to work. Arrangements with friends and co-workers can fall through, leaving us stranded and jeopardizing our job.

In rural areas of developing countries, a woman might walk for eight hours a day just to carry water to her home. Without transportation adults cannot access markets, employment, and basic services that are vital to easing or ending their poverty. In cities children and others walking along congested roads are endangered by traffic and lead-filled exhaust fumes.

What's Fair?

Safe, affordable, and efficient transportation is needed to get everyone moving out of poverty. After a century of use, bicycles are still an economical mode of transportation, used by an estimated 1.4 billion people worldwide. Several developed countries, including the Netherlands, have national bicycle agendas. In addition, a sound transit infrastructure and land use planning and policies are vital. Transportation solutions should increase accessible, affordable, and reliable public transportation systems and energy efficiency while reducing pollution, congestion, and harm to people's health and the environment.

Improving transportation options will enable people to work and protect the environment. UN Millennium Development Goal 7 calls for environmental sustainability.

Imagine This...

Go through your entire day and make note of the types of transportation you use. Now take it away. How would your life change? On whom would you depend? How would you get to work? How would your family fare?

Getting Things Moving

LEARN

☐ Experience firsthand the challenges facing many low-income workers, by using only public transportation every day for a week—not only to travel to work but for all of your transportation needs.

- ☐ Use travel time once a week to read a book or an article about world poverty or to take an action such as writing a letter to a decision maker (if your mode of commuting permits).

- ☐ Read *The Developing World's Motorization Challenge* by Daniel Sperling and Eileen Clausen and note its suggestions for further reading. Also check out transportation-related resources at <**pewclimate.org/orderreport.cfm**>.

- ☐ Link to many environmental organizations through <**envirolink.org**> for practical ideas and tips related to energy and transportation.

CONTRIBUTE

- ☐ Buy extra bus or metro passes and give them to people who ask you for money.

- ☐ Give used bicycles to organizations that repair them for programs serving people who are poor. Visit the International Bicycle Fund <**ibike.org**>, the Bikes Belong Coalition <**bikesbelong.org**>, Pedals for Progress <**p4p.org**>, and similar organizations for more information. Bikes for the World <**bikesfortheworld.org**> provides suggestions for coordinating a bike drive.

- ☐ Donate your frequent-flyer miles to a charity—many of its people need to travel, and you can help. Check with specific airlines for details.

- ☐ Neutralize the negative effects of your driving on climate change by participating in a program that purchases and "retires" greenhouse gas emissions through the Chicago

Climate Exchange greenhouse gas market. DriveNeutral, an enterprise of the San Francisco Presidio School of Management, can help you learn how you can participate **<driveneutral.org>**.

SERVE

- ☐ If you drive to work and have room, arrange to carpool with a co-worker in need of reliable transportation. Ask the human resources department at your workplace about the best way to arrange this.

- ☐ Attend public hearings about your community's public transportation system. Advocate changes that help the lowest-income users and neighborhoods and support cleaner fuel options that benefit everyone.

- ☐ Arrange a partnership between your place of worship and a local social service agency to help transport low-income people to appointments, the grocery store, and other important destinations.

- ☐ Support the Global Lead Initiative **<globalleadnet.org>**, a UN-sponsored campaign to phase out lead-based fuel in countries where it is still used and jeopardizes the health of children and others.

- ☐ Advocate for your mayor to sign the Bike-Friendly Community charter through Vélo Mondial **<velomondial.net>**, an organization working with the United Nations and others to promote cycling as a means of improving air quality and people's health, income, and safety.

A **number of nonprofit** organizations work to repair donated vehicles and distribute them to people in need. For example, the Good News Garage **<goodnewsgarage.org>** in Burlington, Vermont, solicits tax-deductible donations of used cars, trucks, and vans. The garage inspects the vehicles and repairs the best ones, selling three-fourths of them at auction to subsidize operating costs. For the price of repairs (usually less than $1,200), Good News Garage offers the remaining cars, with a thirty-day warranty, to families in need. In 2003 the organization provided 210 cars, most through state-subsidized contracts, to people moving from welfare to work. Other similar programs include Working Wheels in Seattle **<working-wheels.org>** and Driven to Succeed in Detroit.

LIVE

☐ Commit to walking, biking, or taking public transportation to work at least once a week, if you don't already.

☐ Start or join a carpool instead of driving alone.

☐ Explore shared-vehicle options, like Zipcar **<zipcar.com>** or Flexcar **<flexcar.com>**, where you pay a membership fee and then make online reservations to use a car for as little as an hour or for several days. Gas, insurance, and parking are usually included. You may save on insurance, repairs, and other overhead costs associated with car ownership. Some cities have even set aside parking spaces just for shared vehicles. You could use a shared vehicle instead of a second car, or even as your primary car.

☐ Drive a hybrid car **<hybridcar.com>** or convert your vehicle to use an alternative fuel such as waste vegetable oil, straight vegetable oil, or ethanol. See **<journeytoforever.org>** and **<greasecar.com>**.

- ☐ Arrange to telecommute, working from home one or more days a week.
- ☐ Move closer to your job.

Actions Make a Difference

For nearly twenty years, Curitiba, Brazil, has proven the effectiveness of bus rapid transit—systems that typically combine bus lanes, efficient boarding and alighting methods, bus priority at intersections, and station and terminal coordination—resulting in transportation that is high capacity, high speed, and less expensive than rail. Such systems are now found in Quito, Ecuador; São Paulo, Brazil; Nagoya, Japan; Ottawa, Canada; and Pittsburgh, Pennsylvania. *Source: Issues Online in Science and Technology* **<issues.org>**

CHAPTER 20

Travel with a Purpose

Hey, hey, easy kids. Everybody in the car. Boat leaves in two minutes…or perhaps you don't want to see the second-largest ball of twine on the face of the earth, which is only four hours away.

— Chevy Chase, actor, in *National Lampoon's Vacation*

Wish You Were Here

Travel gives us the opportunity to do more than see earth's second-largest ball of twine. It can be a chance to better understand ourselves and our connection to our human family around the globe. Do you remember that first major trip you took and how it changed the way you saw the world and your place in it? Keep looking. Keep traveling.

By traveling to learn and to serve, we can help our world move closer to meeting the UN Millennium Development Goals.

There are now abundant opportunities to take trips for the purpose of connecting with people in other regions, engaging in some form of service, and learning more about global poverty and how it can be resolved. Whether called *insight trips, venture travel, venture philanthropy, volunteer vacations, travel with a purpose,* or some other name, purposeful trips can be transformative for all involved.

"Travel is more than the seeing of sights," reflected author Miriam Beard. "It is a change that goes on, deep and permanent, in the ideas of living." How will your travels change you as you help to change the world?

Imagine This…

If you could travel anywhere in the world to make a difference, where would you go? What kind of work or service would you provide? With whom would you want to travel? Research your dream trip and make it happen.

Traveling for Transformation

LEARN

- ☐ Read a book such as *Volunteer Vacations: Short-term Adventures That Will Benefit You and Others* by Bill McMillan, which contains descriptions of volunteer vacations and lists nearly three hundred organizations. Search *volunteer vacations* on **<barnesandnoble.com>** for other titles.

- ☐ Explore the Web sites of organizations that coordinate volunteer trips. You can find them through the International Volunteer Programs Association **<volunteerinternational.org>**.

- ☐ Contact the national or regional offices of your religious body to find out if they sponsor volunteer vacations, service trips, or travel with a purpose. Some trips are coordinated by the national office; others are arranged by regional bodies or even individual places of worship.

☐ Be a responsible traveler. Be mindful of the impact of tourism on the countries you visit. Is it boosting the local economy? Pushing out people who are poor? Find out as much as you can about the items you purchase. Who made them? Who profits from your purchase? You can arrange a "responsible" holiday through such businesses as **<responsibletravel.com>** and **<transitionsabroad.com>**.

☐ Even if you can't travel, look for ways to learn more about other countries and organizations that are doing great work to reach the UN Millennium Development Goals. To add dimension to your learning, involve your family in reading about other countries, listening to their music, watching documentaries and films about the region, shopping in ethnic markets, and preparing food or eating in restaurants from the culture.

☐ Try out **<googleearth.com>** to visit any place on the planet virtually.

☐ Learn another language so when you travel you can engage with the people and communicate more directly.

CONTRIBUTE

☐ Don't pack light! Before you travel to another country, contact an organization serving others and find out what useful items you can bring to donate.

☐ When abroad, purchase souvenirs, clothing, and other items from local vendors and eat at locally owned restaurants so that your spending directly benefits residents of the communities you visit.

SERVE

- ☐ Plan to participate in a volunteer vacation. Think about the kind of work you would like to do, where you would like to travel, and how much money you can budget. Factors to consider include the organization's track record and references; the trip's work opportunity; your skills, expectations, and experience; security measures; transportation, meals, and accommodations; and what is covered by the cost.

- ☐ You can make a difference close to home by planning a "service vacation" in your own community. You don't even need to travel to gain insights and make an impact.

- ☐ If your place of worship has an annual mission or service trip, participate or help in the planning of other participants' trips.

Fifteen participants in a venture philanthropy vacation visited Save the Children's Adopt-a-Village program in Malawi and climbed Mount Kilimanjaro. Each raised $10,000 for the village program as well as his or her own travel and climbing expenses. After the trip, participants spoke at Save the Children fundraisers and helped raise more than $145,000. One participant reflected afterward, "There's a kid I still see from one of the villages…and I just think, *Is there some way we can help that kid?* We talked about how important it is for us to come to Africa and be ambassadors from the U.S. and show people from that part of the world that there are people from the U.S. who care about them. This is a pure gift.…I felt so much love in those villages and such a sense of community. And I still see their faces every chance I get to daydream. I still feel those kids' hands on me, still sending a surge of electricity through me. So much love and all of it existing in the midst of a horrible AIDS pandemic. Their hope and strength is stunning to behold. It still feels like a dream. The whole trip." *Source: Seattle Times* (August 22, 2004)

☐ Coordinate a campus trip. If you are a college student, faculty member, or administrator, work with a campus service organization to coordinate an "alternative spring break" that will engage students in a service-oriented trip instead of typical spring break revelry.

LIVE

☐ Deepen your usual vacation experience. If you have a regular vacation destination, do some advance research and locate a nearby project or organization serving people in need. Each year plan to take an afternoon or day out of your usual vacation activities and help out.

☐ If you travel overseas on business, add an extra day or two to your trip and arrange to visit or help an organization serving people in need and working to end poverty.

☐ Open your home and family to host a young person participating in an international exchange program.

Actions Make a Difference

Patti and Eliot Daley participated with a half dozen others in a trip to Myanmar (formerly Burma) led by Jack and Lois Young. An art teacher on the trip led an art class with children at an orphanage, using craft supplies the group had brought, while Patti taught the children how to play hackey sack and other ball games. They visited with microcredit entrepreneurs, a doctor establishing a health clinic in an elephant camp, and Burmese youngsters in an English immersion school preparing them for higher-education opportunities. "It was so different than your usual sightseeing tour," reflected Patti after the trip. "It was a people-seeing tour. That is what was so special to me—it was seeing what their lives are like." Trip members learned ways to be of ongoing help and even about opportunities to come back for a ten-month volunteer teaching stint. Two participants donated money so that the children, who were sleeping together on platforms, could have their own beds. "We gained an understanding of how important education and medicine are," Patti reflected, "and what are the most basic areas that make a difference in people's lives."

CHAPTER 21

Save the Lives of Mothers and Newborns

If you want to know the end, look at the beginning.

— African proverb

Healthy Beginnings

Pregnancy and childbirth are, for most, an awe-filled beginning of new life, deeper love, and abundant hope. Of course, there are also those new stretch marks, complete exhaustion, and countless diaper changes! But the last thing we expect is that pregnancy and childbirth will mark an ending—of a mother's life or health, a baby's life, a family's cohesion, or older children's safety and security. Yet each year what should be a wonderful beginning is, indeed, an end. Pregnancy is an end for the more than half a million women who die from pregnancy and childbirth complications, the 20 million who suffer from related illness and injury, the 4 million newborns who die in the first four weeks of life, and the countless millions of their friends and family members.

A Good Start

We can do better—for babies in Burundi, mothers in Malawi, siblings in Sierra Leone, and families in Afghanistan. *All* pregnant women need access to prenatal care; a skilled attendant; a clean delivery; a timely referral and access to responsive, high-quality emergency care when needed; as well as followup care for themselves and their babies. Three million babies' lives could be saved every year by existing, low-tech, low-cost measures such as breastfeeding, being kept warm, and two $0.20 tetanus vaccines for their mothers when pregnant.

Improving maternal and newborn health creates a future full of promise. UN Millennium Development Goal 5 includes a target of reducing by three-quarters the maternal mortality rate.

Solutions involve more than improving the health-care system. Helping girls stay in school increases their chances of better understanding how to be healthier, and it often delays pregnancies. Improving transportation, communication, incomes, and access to clean water and sanitation is also key. Finally, by better understanding and tackling the complex social, cultural, economic, and political challenges to the status of women, we can save the lives of women in pregnancy and childbirth and those of their babies.

Imagine This...

Imagine not naming your new baby until she is several weeks old because the odds are high that she might not survive, as is customary in some developing countries. Now imagine babies in Niger named Zoé ("Life") because her mother got a tetanus vaccine, René ("Reborn") because his mother had a skilled birth attendant who recognized and acted when emergency care was needed and his life was in jeopardy, and Aimée ("Loved") who lived despite her tiny size because her mother was encouraged to breastfeed her and keep her warm. Imagine babies named Victoire ("Victory") because we did all we could to improve the chances of mothers and babies everywhere.

Undertaking a Labor of Love

LEARN

- ☐ Visit Save the Children **<savethechildren.org>** to learn more about its Saving Newborn Lives program and read the links to informative resources such as the executive summary of the Lancet Neonatal Survival Series.
- ☐ Read "Accelerating Reductions in Maternal and Newborn Mortality," a report from the Global Women's Action Network for Children gathering, at **<childrensdefense.org>**. Read about the organization's efforts on maternal health and newborn health. Sign up for its newsletter to stay informed.
- ☐ Check out the White Ribbon Alliance **<whiteribbon alliance.org>** to learn more about how the group is bringing together organizations large and small to address maternal mortality.
- ☐ See chapters 2, 5, and 22 on education, children's health, and clean water for ways to improve these areas that have such an impact on maternal and newborn health.

> *"My eldest daughter died of postpartum hemorrhage four years ago. In this project we are saving women's lives with misoprostol. If we had had this earlier, we would have saved her life, too."*
>
> — Margaum, traditional Tanzanian midwife, Venture Strategies for Health and Development **<venturestrategies.org>**

CONTRIBUTE

- ☐ Honor a new mother by making a gift in her baby's name to an organization working to save the lives of mothers and babies.

- ☐ Celebrate Mother's Day by donating in a mother's name to an organization mentioned here, instead of spending money on flowers or a restaurant meal.

- ☐ Donate baby-care items to organizations serving low-income families.

- ☐ Pass on your books and magazines about parenting and child care for the waiting rooms of health clinics and organizations serving new mothers.

- ☐ Give to organizations such as the Fistula Foundation **<fistulafoundation.org>** that are helping women who suffer childbirth complications regain their health and dignity.

SERVE

- ☐ Advocate for greater assistance to developing countries to improve their water, health-care, education, and transportation systems. Save the Children's Advocacy Center offers advocacy information and support to help make your voice heard.

- ☐ Serve in a medically underserved community as a health professional or a volunteer.

- ☐ Volunteer with a home visitor program supporting new, at-risk mothers to offer advice, encouragement, and referrals to other resources.

It's called "kangaroo care." In Malawi, where twenty thousand mothers watch their newborns die each year, babies' lives are now being saved by this simple technique to keep babies, especially premature ones, warm by maintaining skin-to-skin contact with their mothers. It doesn't cost big bucks or use complicated technology—just vital know-how that Save the Children and others are spreading to save the youngest and smallest babies.

☐ Arrange a partnership between your place of worship and a community health clinic to provide transportation to help pregnant women and new mothers attend medical appointments.

LIVE

☐ Honor women everywhere. Always.

Actions Make a Difference

Honduras nearly cut in half the deaths of women in childbirth in just six years by establishing hospitals and rural health centers; increasing the number of skilled staff; mobilizing community support for women during pregnancy, at childbirth, and postpartum; and providing reproductive health services.

CHAPTER 22

Improve Access to Clean Water

If there is magic on this planet, it is contained in water.

— Loren Eiseley, anthropologist, author

More Than Just a Drop in the Bucket

Don't you hate dripping faucets? Listening to that aggravating *drip-drip-drip* may be the most thought we give to the water in our lives. With water available at the turn of a faucet to fill a glass, brush our teeth, flush the toilet, or take a shower, to most of us having clean and abundant water is a given.

That's not the case, however, for the 1 billion people around the globe who lack safe drinking water. Of every ten people worldwide, only about five have a piped water supply in their home or yard; three use a protected well, a public standpipe, or some other improved water supply; and two must rely on potentially unsafe water from rivers, ponds, unprotected wells, or water vendors. More than 2.5 billion people don't even have access to a simple "improved" latrine.

"Though some analysts have predicted future conflicts over water, many countries successfully share river basins, inland seas, and other water resources, showing this challenge can also be a powerful catalyst for international cooperation."

— Kofi Annan, former secretary general of the United Nations

Pouring Ourselves into Making a Difference

Each action we take to make safe drinking water and sanitation accessible to all will be more than just a drop in the bucket. It will reduce health costs and disease, especially diarrhea, and also save time—increasing work, school attendance, and even relaxation.

Access to clean water and sanitation is essential to eliminating poverty. UN Millennium Development Goal 7 includes a target of reducing by half by 2015 the proportion of people without sustainable access to safe drinking water and basic sanitation.

"When the well is dry," wrote Benjamin Franklin, "we know the worth of water." When people around the world are healthy, better educated, and living dramatically improved lives because of access to clean water, we will know the value of our actions.

Imagine This...

If you were a woman living in a developing country, chances are you'd be walking, on average, six to nine miles every day just to collect water. "In South Africa alone, women and children collectively walk the equivalent distance of sixteen times to the moon and back per day, gathering water for families," reports the United Nations Development Fund for Women **<unifem.org>**. If you didn't have to spend an average of eight hours a day collecting water, you could be growing and preparing food, engaging in income-generating work, or attending school. Imagine the difference it would make.

Tapping into Our Commitment

LEARN

- ☐ Gather a group of friends, neighbors, colleagues, or members of your place of worship to watch and discuss *One Water,* a twenty-minute film about the state of drinkable water in the world **<onewater.org>**. Relate this to water use in your community.

- ☐ Read *A Cool Drink of Water* by Barbara Kerley to children and discuss what you learn.

- ☐ With your kids, watch the video *Splish and Splash.* And with your adult friends, view *Water: The Drop of Life.* Both are available at **<un.org/waterforlifedecade>**.

- ☐ Watch *The Diary of Jay-Z: Water for Life.* The film is available at MTV's Web site **<waterforlife.mtv.com>**.

- ☐ Ask your schools to present the story of how water comes into the homes and schools of your community. Invite the local public utility director to be a guest speaker.

> *"For now,...there's no better way to protect our planet's water supply than to use less water....In the United States, we use water at about twice the rate of other industrialized nations. The bulk of U.S. water usage goes toward agriculture—about 70 to 80 percent. But at home approximately 74 percent of our water usage is in the bathroom. The amount of water we use there can easily be reduced with only a little thought."*
>
> — John M. Fahey Jr., President and CEO, National Geographic Society

- ☐ Watch and discuss with friends *An Inconvenient Truth* **<theclimateproject.org>**, Al Gore's documentary, to better understand how global warming is affecting our globe's water cycle.

- ☐ Make a presentation about global water needs to a community, business, neighborhood, or religious group, using the PowerPoint presentation and other materials from Water for People **<waterforpeople.org/educate.html>**. You can join one of the organization's many community groups to participate in a variety of outreach, fund-raising, and education events.

- ☐ Engage students in learning more about water worldwide, using the educational resources provided by WaterPartners International **<water.org>**.

- ☐ Find out how your community compares with others in your region in terms of water consumption. Do you consume more water, that is, waste it? Is your wastewater cleaned before it goes back into the water table? What are the sources of pollution in the water around you? Are there water meters?

- ☐ Talk up the fact that water bottles can and must be refilled—at the tap—in most places in our own world. Do it.

Laughter may be the loudest sound you'll hear at rural African schools with a PlayPump, an innovative water pump doubling as a children's merry-go-round that is bringing clean water—and a better life—to hundreds of thousands of families in Africa. As children spin on a merry-go-round, water pumps from below the ground and is stored in a nearby tank, making safe water available in the community. Nearly seven hundred PlayPumps have been installed in South Africa, providing safe water to 1 million people. Thousands more PlayPumps will be installed throughout sub-Saharan Africa, bringing accessible, clean water to millions more.

☐ Make a family decision to not waste water in your home. Talk about how that can be done. See ways under "Live" that might inspire you.

CONTRIBUTE

☐ Support the work of the Carter Center **<cartercenter.org>** to eradicate Guinea worm disease, river blindness, and other waterborne illnesses.

☐ Raise funds to contribute to an organization making clean water and sanitation accessible in the developing world.

☐ Involve children in selling lemonade and other drinks on hot days and donate the profits to a clean-water organization. Prepare simple fact sheets about the need for clean water worldwide and invite donations above the cost of drinks.

☐ Involve a class or other group in pledging a certain amount of money (such as a dime or a dollar) every time they use clean water over the course of a day or week. Have the students research clean-water nonprofits and donate the proceeds to the organization of their choice.

SERVE

☐ See chapter 11 for ways to support microcredit, which often helps borrowers install sanitary latrines and improve their access to clean water.

☐ Visit **<playpumps.org>** to find out how you can support its work to install PlayPumps to bring clean water (and fun) to schools and communities in Africa. You can download a flyer to spread the word to others. Work to involve your school, workplace, civic or scouting group, place of worship, or other organization, or make a donation toward the $10,000 cost of each PlayPump.

- ☐ Find out about new environmentally based ways of cleaning water, such as reed beds and artificial wetlands. Agitate for using one of these in your community to clean organic wastes naturally.

- ☐ Organize with others to urge a municipal ordinance against using drinking water to water lawns, wash vehicles, and hose down sidewalks; see if "gray water" could be used instead.

- ☐ Advocate for policies and programs that will increase clean-water access worldwide and make your voice heard to work for systemic change on a global scale. Connect with WaterAid <**wateraid.org**> and other organizations providing advocacy support.

- ☐ Plan a family, school, or community observance of World Water Day, celebrated each year on March 22. Learn more about the International Decade for Action in "Water for Life," sponsored by the United Nations.

LIVE

- ☐ Appreciate water as a valuable resource and conserve it—even if you live in a community with abundant lakes and rivers. It costs money and resources—and disrupts nature—to gather, store, transport, purify, monitor, and deliver water, so cut down on unnecessary use. Actions to conserve water in your daily life include:
    - Installing a low-flow faucet aerator, available from a hardware store

- Turning off the faucet while brushing teeth and shaving
- Washing the car with a bucket instead of a running hose
- Installing a new low-flow toilet that uses less water or putting a water displacement device in an older toilet's tank
- Purchasing a rainwater collection device.

☐ Eat more meatless meals and use less paper. Livestock and paper production are major water users.

☐ Drink tap water instead of bottled water—all the time. Calculate what you have typically spent on bottled water each year and make an annual contribution in that amount to a clean-water organization. (You'll also help the environment by eliminating plastic bottles.) Bottle your own tap water when you need portable, potable water!

☐ Prevent pollution of groundwater and surface water. Dispose of hazardous waste (such as paint) appropriately. Many communities have hazardous-waste collections on designated dates in specified locations.

Actions Make a Difference

Reaching the target of UN Millennium Development Goal 7 for water and sanitation will save between $3 and $34 for every dollar invested, according to the World Health Organization.

CHAPTER 23

Increase International Development Aid

The test of our progress is not whether we add more to the abundance of those who have much; it is whether we provide enough for those who have little.

— FRANKLIN DELANO ROOSEVELT,
U.S. PRESIDENT, 1933–1945

Small Change

At the end of the day, do you empty your pockets of the change that accumulated over the day—a couple of quarters after you bought a coffee or a newspaper, what was left over from the dollar you put in the vending machine, the change the clerk at the drugstore gave you? We don't give much thought to the small change. Maybe we slip it into our pockets when we get dressed the next day; or we drop the coins into a jar until the collection gets really big and then we convert it into bills at the bank.

By working together we can increase aid for international development by 1 percent of the federal budget to help meet UN Millennium Development Goal 8: to develop a global partnership for development, with a target of more-generous official assistance for countries committed to poverty reduction.

Now consider a different kind of change—one that could save lives, improve health, increase education, raise incomes, and protect the environment. The change championed by the ONE Campaign **<one.org>** (spearheaded by rock star Bono and a number of national organizations) is to increase U.S. foreign-aid assistance by 1 percent of the U.S.

federal budget, or roughly $25 billion. The UN Millennium Project estimates that it will take an additional $75 billion annually of investment in developing countries to meet the UN Millennium Development Goals by 2015. Over the past thirteen years, the United States has only once given more than 0.2 percent. But we could provide our share by increasing U.S. foreign aid by just one penny of every dollar in the federal budget. That's change that will make a positive, lifesaving difference!

Imagine This...

What if, in addition to our government's meeting the goal of 1 percent, citizens and small and corporate business also committed the equivalent of their pocket change? What if we led the way by each giving 1 percent of our income to aid those suffering the worst effects of poverty?

Making Change

LEARN

- ☐ Access the Web sites of the ONE Campaign **<one.org>**, DATA **<data.org>**, and the UN Millennium Project **<unmillenniumproject.org>** to learn more.

- ☐ Learn more about foreign aid and debt relief. Download *Paying the Price*, a report by Oxfam International **<oxfam.org>**, which describes challenges and solutions for foreign aid and debt forgiveness and their role in meeting the UN Millennium Development Goals.

- ☐ Gather with friends to watch the Emmy Award–winning HBO movie *The Girl in the Café* (2005) for a light but thought-provoking introduction to this massive political challenge.

- ☐ Engage your religious congregation in studying the UN Millennium Development Goals and making a faithful response to help meet them. Churches can use the National Council of Churches' six-session study guide available at **<ncccusa.org>**.

CONTRIBUTE

- ☐ Save your pocket change and donate it to a global poverty organization. Or donate 1 percent of your household budget, or of your income, to poverty-alleviating organizations.

- ☐ Support the Millennium Villages, which are demonstrating the power and the possibility of reaching the UN Millennium Development Goals **<millenniumpromise.org>**.

> ***"We have the opportunity in the coming decade to cut world poverty by half. Billions more people could enjoy the fruits of the global economy. Tens of millions of lives can be saved. The practical solutions exist. The political framework is established. And, for the first time, the cost is utterly affordable. Whatever one's motivation for attacking the crisis of extreme poverty—human rights, religious values, security, fiscal prudence, ideology—the solutions are the same. All that is needed is action."***
>
> — UN Millennium Project

Aid works. According to *Paying the Price,* by Oxfam International, millions of children are in school in Tanzania, Uganda, Kenya, Malawi, and Zambia thanks to money provided by debt relief and foreign aid. For the same reason, Ugandans no longer have to pay for basic health care, a policy that resulted in an increase of 50 to 100 percent in attendance at Ugandan health clinics and doubled the rate of immunizations. Roads built with foreign aid mean that Ethiopian farmers can reach local and international markets to sell their crops more efficiently, children in rural areas can travel to schools more easily, and people can reach hospitals more quickly—which is often a critical factor affecting maternal and infant mortality rates. In Bolivia financial support to indigenous peoples has amplified their political voice—in particular to support women's groups to monitor local government's implementation of policies to promote equality for women and men. Key demands such as protection against sexual violence and improved standards of reproductive-health care have now been included in local government plans.

To meet the Millennium Development Goals, we need not only *more* foreign aid but also *better* foreign aid so that the money that is given is used more efficiently and effectively. Both the donor countries and the developing countries have responsibilities for making the aid work better. Donors must focus more on poverty reduction and less on using aid as a political tool. They must reduce the management burden, conditions, and uncertainty of aid delivery that often accompany aid. The recipients must combat corruption and build strong and accountable public sectors. They have to provide secure delivery systems and staffing necessary for people to receive the help; and they must ensure that governments, civil society, and the media serve as watchdogs to monitor public spending and prevent corruption. If we all do our part, our aid will be more than just a band-aid and can lead to strong, long-term solutions.

SERVE

- ☐ Sign the ONE declaration at **<one.org>**.
- ☐ E-mail friends and encourage them to sign the ONE declaration.
- ☐ Put a ONE Campaign banner on your Web site.
- ☐ Contact your community's elected leaders and urge them to name your community a "City of ONE." Recruit others to join you in building public support for this declaration.
- ☐ E-mail the president and urge the leaders of our nation to donate its "pocket change" by increasing foreign aid by 1 percent of the federal budget.
- ☐ Speak out as a champion for the United States' meeting the ONE goal. Connect with a ONE Campaign partner organization that provides advocacy information, resources, and support **<one.org/partners>**.
- ☐ Commit to building relationships with influential leaders within your own community to help them become champions for making poverty history and achieving the UN Millennium Development Goals.

LIVE

- ☐ Wear a white wristband to indicate your support for the ONE Campaign to Make Poverty History. Raise awareness by talking to people about what it stands for.

☐ Visit a developing country and arrange to see, firsthand, the difference that foreign aid has made in improving the lives of those who are poor.

Actions Make a Difference

Working with the Earth Institute at Columbia University and the UN Millennium Project, at least seventy-five Millennium Villages have sprung up in ten African countries. Impoverished villages in Ethiopia, Ghana, Kenya, Malawi, Mali, Nigeria, Rwanda, Senegal, Tanzania, and Uganda are using proven, powerful, and practical technologies bundled into straightforward solutions and backed by a comprehensive investment strategy.

Millennium Promise **<millenniumpromise.org>** invests in health, education, food production, access to clean water, and essential infrastructure so that these community-led interventions will enable impoverished villages to escape extreme poverty once and for all. Once these communities get a foothold on the bottom rung of the development ladder, they can propel themselves on a path of self-sustaining economic growth.

CHAPTER 24

Speak Up for Justice

More Thoughts on Advocacy

Private charity is no substitute for public justice.

— Marian Wright Edelman, founder and president of the Children's Defense Fund

You Have a Voice

"To stay quiet," wrote author and political activist Arundhati Roy, "is as political an act as speaking out." Why is it that we tend to keep quiet on political topics instead of speaking up for what we think is right? Are we afraid of offending others or of being criticized? Do we feel like it wouldn't make a difference? Is the whole legislative process too confusing or intimidating? Do we think we need to know more before we speak up?

> *"It is not the kings and the generals but the masses of the people that make history."*
>
> — Nelson Mandela, South African civil rights leader and former president of South Africa

What if we just decided to do it: to speak up and speak out on the big issues that affect our nation and our world? What if we determined to be powerful voices for the end of poverty in our day? What if we embraced our power?

Hour by hour, day by day, each of us can act to end poverty and instill hope for tomorrow. Reaching out and taking action through hands-on service makes an immediate difference. Giving money, goods, and time all help improve lives close at hand and around the world. As valuable and needed as these forms of action are, advocacy is one of the most important things we can do in our work to overcome poverty. Changing the world and ending poverty require that we speak out about injustice and advocate to create more-just systems, policies, and practices.

Through persistent advocacy on every level, people ended slavery, apartheid, and segregation—even though many thought they would never be abolished. In the United States, women won the right to vote, every child got the right to a free public education, and children no longer were forced to work—all because people organized. From a solitary whisper to a collective shout, when we join our voices we can change systems, end injustice, and transform the world.

Tips for Writing a Letter to Elected Officials or Other Decision-makers

1. Introduce yourself.
2. Describe the problem you are concerned about, drawing on firsthand experience or examples if possible.
3. Share your vision for what is needed.
4. Urge the official's leadership in taking a specific action to solve the problem.
5. Describe the positive impact such an action could have.
6. Ask for a reply indicating what he or she will do.
7. Sign your name (legibly, if handwritten), with contact information.
8. Be polite, brief, and timely (writing just before a critical vote, for instance).

9. You can fax, e-mail, or mail your letter. For contact information for U.S. representatives and senators, go to **<house.gov>** and **<senate.gov>**.

10. Once you've taken the time to write to the decision-maker, you can easily adapt your letter to be a letter to the editor of the local paper, which will greatly increase the number of people who hear your call to action—and it may inspire them to do the same.

11. Invite others to write letters with you. Advocacy has the greatest impact when done as part of a coalition of constituents speaking out on the same issue. Join an advocacy group, perhaps one listed in this book, to coordinate your efforts.

Make Your Voice Heard

Decide to Network

Use every letter you write

Every conversation you have

Every meeting you attend

To express your fundamental beliefs and dreams.

Affirm to others the vision of the world you want.

Network through thought

Network through action

Network through love

Network through the spirit.

You are the center of a network

You are the center of the world

You are a free, immensely powerful source of life and goodness.

Affirm it.
Spread it.
Radiate it.
Think day and night about it
And you will see a miracle happen:
The greatness of your own life.
In a world of big powers, media, and monopolies
But of [6 billion] individuals
Networking is the new freedom
The new democracy
A new form of happiness.

— Robert Muller, former UN assistant secretary general and author of *Most of All They Taught Me Happiness* <robertmuller.org>

Imagine This…

Some years ago National Public Radio reported that two long-distance phone companies in Florida were named "I Don't Care" and "It Doesn't Matter." When new local phone service customers were asked which long-distance company they wanted, those who replied "I don't care" or "It doesn't matter" unwittingly were signed up for these companies. Whenever we fail to vote in an election or don't tell our elected leaders our opinions on priorities, problems, solutions, and legislation, we are in effect signing up for "I Don't Care" and "It Doesn't Matter."

Imagine instead signing up with an advocacy organization to become a concerned citizen leader who communicates regularly with your elected representatives, weighing in on urgent national and international priorities and building public support for solutions you urge them to put in place. Imagine inspiring your elected leaders to become champions for the end of poverty. Imagine signing up for "I Care About Ending Poverty" and "Our World Matters."

Joining Others for Justice

LEARN

☐ Appreciate the potential power of your own existing network. Jot down a list of formal and informal groups to which you belong (extended family, religious congregation, neighbors, individuals in your e-mail address book, co-workers, health club, parents' group) and the number of people in each.

☐ Brainstorm ways you can communicate with and engage these groups—newsletters, e-mails, letters, flyers, phone calls, bulletin boards, meetings, and so forth. Whom might you naturally enlist to partner with you as you begin or extend your advocacy efforts?

☐ Refer to this list as you work for justice in our world. Use your network for support, to get others involved, to spread the word to their own networks, and more. You already have a bigger sphere of influence than you might have realized!

☐ Find out who your elected officials are: their names, e-mail addresses, and phone numbers. Visit **<house.gov>** and **<senate.gov>** and the Web sites of your city and county. Keep the information accessible in your e-mail address book, traditional address book, or on your refrigerator. They are representing you—that's their job; make sure they know where you stand!

☐ Read practical and inspiring books on grassroots organizing and advocacy, such as *Stick Your Neck Out: A Street-smart Guide to Creating Change in Your Community* by John Graham; *Reclaiming Our Democracy: Healing the Break Between People and Government* by Sam Daley-Harris; and *Organizing for Social Change: Midwest Academy Manual for Activists* by Kimberley A. Bobo, Steve Max, and Jackie Kendall. Encourage others to read and discuss them with you and make an action plan.

☐ Bring a child with you when you vote. Involving children in this way educates them about the democratic process and encourages them to vote when they are of age. Encourage schools to teach children about voting—perhaps even arranging for a polling-machine demonstration so they can practice using it.

☐ Sign up for an e-mail newsletter from an organization working for systemic change to end poverty and make our world more just. Most national religious bodies have them (e.g., Religious Action Center of Reform Judaism, the National Council of the Churches of Christ, and many denominations and faith groups). Or sign up for one from an organization working on a particular aspect of poverty or other issue of concern (e.g., Bread for the World, the Children's Defense Fund, the Global Health Campaign, Jubilee USA, and the Microcredit Summit Campaign) or a multi-issue electronic advocacy group (such as the ONE Campaign and Millennium Promise). E-mail contact information is available on the individual organizations' Web sites.

☐ Attend a conference hosted by one of the organizations working on advocating for justice in the United States and around the world. Many include lobby days so you can experience advocating to your senators and representatives with the support and the company of others.

- ☐ Engage your place of worship, or a group within it, in exploring the religious texts and teachings that call for justice for those who are poor, hungry, and oppressed. In light of that study, explore what your place of worship is doing and what more it could do to fulfill that mandate. Many religious traditions and denominations have curriculum materials and other study resources focused on justice and poverty. In addition, Bread for the World **<bread.org>** has two resources: "Hunger No More" and "Biblical Basics for Justice." The National Council of Churches has a curriculum on the UN Millennium Development Goals, and the Children's Defense Fund prepares annual study and worship materials on seeking justice for poor and disadvantaged children in the United States.

CONTRIBUTE

- ☐ Contribute time and money to the campaigns of candidates who have demonstrated their commitment to ending poverty in the United States and around the world.

- ☐ Donate to grassroots advocacy organizations that are working effectively to end poverty. Because their work creating political pressure means that contributions are not tax-deductible, grassroots lobbying organizations usually can't count on foundation and corporate grants and rely on individual donations.

SERVE

- ☐ Register to vote—and vote!

- ☐ Attend town hall meetings, community forums, and other opportunities to ask questions, raise concerns about poverty, and urge leadership in finding solutions. Bring a friend for support and to double your impact.

- ☐ Participate in or organize marches, demonstrations, and other gatherings intended to highlight public concern about global poverty and increase the demand for solutions.

- ☐ Join up with a group doing voter registration to enable all people, especially those who are poor, to make their voices heard; vote for leaders with a commitment to ending poverty.

- ☐ Adopt a legislator. Forge relationships with your senators and representatives and keep them informed on global poverty-related concerns. Arrange to meet with representatives when they are in their district offices (much more effective than trying to meet with them in Washington, D.C., where many tourist groups troop through). If it is your first time and you need moral support, find a friend or colleague who has done it before to accompany you. Write letters on issues of importance. Call your representatives when a vote on legislation is coming up. Send them copies of letters to the editor and op-eds from your local newspaper that support your concerns. Encourage others to contact them too.

- ☐ Make your voice heard. Call in to radio programs that address topics related to global poverty to inform, inspire, and urge others to act.

- ☐ Join a group that provides ongoing support to activists working for justice on global and U.S. poverty, health, and other issues. The support of others is crucial to providing the encouragement and support that most of us need to take on and sustain this sometimes-daunting commitment. Not only is it more fun to work with others, but the more people who are involved in a coordinated effort, the greater the impact.
- ☐ Volunteer with an election watch group.
- ☐ Watch *Washington Journal* on C-SPAN, *Washington Week in Review,* and similar programs for information on upcoming legislation and other political matters.

LIVE

- ☐ Run for public office.
- ☐ Explore serving on the board of directors, or in another capacity, of a nonprofit organization that is working to end poverty.
- ☐ Travel and stand with people in other countries who are gaining the right to vote and speak out.

Actions Make a Difference

How could Sam Harris end world hunger and poverty? He was just a music teacher. But then he realized that his discouragement wasn't about a lack of solutions for ending hunger and poverty; he was hopeless about human nature—that we would never put the solutions in place. He realized that he could control one person's actions—his own. So he started by presenting programs to high school students on what they could do to end world hunger. He asked if they knew the name of their congressional representatives. (He learned that only about two hundred out of seven thousand did.) Sam founded a grassroots citizen lobby—RESULTS **<results.org>**—to create the political will to end hunger and poverty, providing information, skills, and support to help ordinary people find their voices as citizen activists. In the thirty years since Sam's first epiphany, RESULTS citizen advocates have helped raise billions of dollars of foreign aid, which has been directed into basic health and microcredit programs, resulting in saving millions of lives and helping millions more people move out of poverty.

Conclusion

Dream of a Bright Tomorrow

A vision without a task is but a dream. A task without vision is drudgery. A vision and a task is the hope of the world.

— INSCRIPTION, CHURCH IN SUSSEX, ENGLAND, 1730

It's time now to dream, knowing we have a collective vision and the tasks to accomplish it: together we can end poverty. If you've read the whole book, you will have encountered more than four hundred actions and you'll be mulling them over for many days to come. Which seem right for you? Sleep on these ideas, discuss them with a friend, jot down your thoughts on paper, work them out during a run—and then spin out a dream of the difference you would like to make. Whatever you do, though, don't put this book back on your shelf! At least keep it on your nightstand as a reminder that tomorrow will dawn, new and bright, and we'll have another day to make a real difference.

Take a minute now to close your eyes and envision the world you would like to see in 2015—or sooner. Imagine the faces of children around the world and hear their laughter. See the fields abundant with harvest; taste the rice or cornmeal or other produce that provides families with enough to eat. Hear the splash of plentiful, clean water. Smell the rich aroma of coffee produced by workers paid a fair wage, or the tortillas cooked by a

> ***"I learned this, at least, by my experiment: that if one advances confidently in the direction of his dreams, and endeavors to live the life which he has imagined, he will meet with a success unexpected in common hours."***
>
> — HENRY DAVID THOREAU, AMERICAN WRITER, PHILOSOPHER, AND NATURALIST

micro-entrepreneur now able to provide for her family. Imagine opening the doors of classrooms around the world and seeing every young child, eyes bright with curiosity, eager to learn. Feel the comforting touch of a health-care provider's hand, and know that care is available for every woman, man, and child when they are sick and to keep them well. Hear the *whirr* of bicycle wheels transporting workers or the quiet hum of public transportation using alternative fuel; breathe in the fresh air unpolluted by lead-based exhaust. Touch the sturdy walls of a house—cool corrugated iron or mud, brick, or wood. Enjoy its strong protection. Is this a dream? Or can this be our reality?

Bright Tomorrows

> *When our days become dreary with low-hovering clouds of despair, and when our nights become darker than a thousand midnights, let us remember that there is a creative force in this universe, working to pull down the gigantic mountains of evil, a power that is able to make a way out of no way and transform dark yesterdays into bright tomorrows. Let us realize the arc of the moral universe is long but it bends toward justice.*
>
> — DR. MARTIN LUTHER KING JR., *WHERE DO WE GO FROM HERE: CHAOS OR COMMUNITY?*

When he spoke these words, Dr. King knew the day had come to end segregation, even though at times it had looked impossible. So too we know that the day has come to put an end to poverty in our world, which has the resources, tools, and know-how to accomplish it. There will be nights when we fall into bed exhausted by the enormity of the challenge or just by the demands of our everyday lives. But there will also be nights when we get ready for bed, knowing that something we did that day moved our world just a little bit closer to the end of poverty.

Together we can be astronomers, whose fingers trace the arc of the moral universe, bending toward justice. Our North Star is the goal of ending poverty in our world. We will keep our eyes on the UN Millennium Development Goals until they are reached: extreme hunger and poverty are eradicated; all children, boys and girls alike, complete primary school; women and girls have equality and are empowered; child deaths are reduced; mothers' and newborns' health is improved; HIV/AIDS, malaria, and other diseases are combated; we have achieved environmental sustainability and provided clean water, sanitation, and housing for all; and there are global partnerships for development.

These are not just dreams that will disappear in the morning. They beckon us to lives of vision and commitment to create bright hope for tomorrow.

Resources

How to Use This Book with Others

The following guides suggest ways to use *Our Day to End Poverty* in group settings: schools, workplaces, and places of worship.

Questions to ask in discussing the chapters with others include:

- What creates hope?
- What inspires action?
- What makes a difference?
- What dampens hope, and how can that be overcome?
- What inhibits action, and how can that be overcome?
- What diminishes making a difference?
- What is your vision for the world?
- What would you do if you were positive that it would make a difference—that you would succeed? In what ways does fear of failure inhibit our actions to end poverty?
- Do you think we can eliminate poverty? Why or why not?
- Who bears responsibility for ending poverty in our world?
- What is poverty? What creates poverty? What perpetuates poverty?
- What do you think is required to eradicate poverty?
- What would motivate or sustain your efforts to end poverty in our day?
- What values do you hold that shape your feelings and actions about ending poverty?
- What are you already doing that is helping bring an end to poverty?
- What is one new step you will take to help eliminate poverty? What tools or support do you need?

Our Day to End Poverty: Guide for Schools

This book could be used as a resource for:

- Classroom lessons
- Assemblies (e.g., on World Water Day, World Food Day, or other awareness days noted in the book)
- Service-learning requirements/programs
- Social action clubs
- Small-group independent study or research projects

Options include:

- Presenting a lesson on the topic in one chapter and having students select actions to take or further learning to pursue, drawing on the books, videos, Web sites, and other resources suggested
- Having individual students or small groups select different chapters to read, learn more about, and present to the rest of the class, club, or school
- Organizing a multisession study based on several or all of the chapters
- Incorporating information and actions from the book into your standard curriculum for social studies, science, math, language arts, history, or other subjects

Our Day to End Poverty: Guide for the Workplace

Find ways to bring *Our Day to End Poverty* to your workplace. Possibilities include:

- A brown-bag lunch at which you or an invited speaker introduces the topic and opportunities for action and facilitates discussion
- An all-staff meeting
- Purchasing and distributing copies to the staff
- A breakfast book club that reads and discusses the chapters in succession
- Instituting a service program in which staff members are released for a certain number of hours per week to engage in volunteer activities
- Discussing with senior management ways to respond/contribute as a company or an organization to the end of poverty in our day
- Exploring with human resources ways to implement ideas in the book that will improve the well-being of employees (such as transportation, child care, and health care)

Questions for group discussion and individual reflection in the workplace:

- What values does our workplace hold that support ending poverty?
- What does our workplace already do to help end poverty (e.g., provide health care coverage, offer child-care assistance, pay a living wage)?

- What resources does our company possess (physical resources such as the building or product, human resources, and also intangible resources like visibility and influence) that we could contribute to help end poverty in our day?
- What are the costs and the benefits to our workplace of taking collective or individual actions to end poverty?
- How can our workplace actively support individual or collective action?
- What changes would be required for employees to take action individually or collectively? Who has the power to put them in place?

Our Day to End Poverty: Guide for Places of Worship

First decide whom you would like to engage with *Our Day to End Poverty* in your place of worship. Options include:

- Religious education classes of either adults or young people
- Existing small groups such as a youth group, women's group, men's group, or young adults group
- Existing committees, such as social concerns, outreach, or missions, or a joint meeting of several existing committees
- A new class, group, or committee convened around this topic
- The congregation as a whole
- Other congregations in your community

Second, consider how you would like to engage others in the book.

- **Multiweek study.** Have participants read one chapter in advance, then discuss the actions together. Maintain a running list of actions the group is interested in pursuing together. At the end of the study, prioritize the actions and get started.
- **Afternoon forum.** Divide into small groups and have each group read and discuss actions that they are most inspired to take individually or collectively. Reconvene as a large group and share what was learned. Or invite a speaker or panel of speakers to present the topic—including opportunities to take action—so that participants leave not only informed but also committed to act.
- **Weekend retreat.** Invite a knowledgeable speaker or speakers to present the topic and facilitate discussion.

- **Summer service/mission trip.** Use the book to learn more about a problem and a solution that the group would like to engage in and to prepare members for effective service.
- **Worship.** Lift up the problems and a call to action in worship. This could include anything from focusing an entire worship service on one or more of the concerns in the book (hunger, for example, or housing). Or, your place of worship could commit to including a focus on these concerns in each service, through a prayer, announcement, or bulletin insert with information and options for action.
- **Congregational displays.** In a central location, such as a fellowship or assembly hall, designate a bulletin board or other area to display information and action opportunities to help end poverty in our nation and our world. In addition to information from this book, post photos, newspaper articles, success stories, and other materials that will inform and inspire.

However you plan to use this book, you may want to take the following steps:

- Secure permission or support from appropriate leaders, staff, or committees, if necessary.
- Contact a national office of your religious tradition or denomination to discover the resources it has prepared on any or all of the topics in this book. Resources may be available through the religious education, social concerns, international service, and public policy staff of your religious tradition.
- In addition to resources specifically prepared to address global hunger and poverty, draw on sacred texts; resources on justice, ethics, and community; hymns and other sacred

music related to the themes; and the lives of religious figures in your tradition to illuminate your study and discussions.

- Invite speakers, when appropriate, to present the topic and facilitate the discussion. Members of your religious community may serve as knowledgeable speakers on specific topics.
- Explore any volunteer programs, funds, agencies, or other efforts sponsored by your religious tradition to respond to the needs identified in the book; consider how your place of worship can support them as an outcome of its study.

Index

K

L

T

U

V

W

Y

Z

About the Book Team

Our Day to End Poverty is the result of a uniquely collaborative process. The "book team" comprised five of us, each with a particular but dynamic role. Jeff Keenan, after witnessing the juxtaposition of prosperity and poverty while working in Asia, sought to discern the contribution he could make to help end poverty. He engaged in conversation with Joy Anderson, president and founder of Criterion Ventures, about the roles individuals play in social change. They realized that there was a need for the global poverty equivalent of the environmental book *50 Simple Things You Can Do to Save the Earth* by the EarthWorks Group. Joy set about assembling a team. Shannon Daley-Harris came on board to write the book, drawing on her decades of U.S. and international work with and on behalf of children. Karen Speerstra, a longtime publisher, joined the team to edit the book. Jackie VanderBrug, Criterion Ventures' managing director, brought insight and ideas to the process and the book's form and content.

Operating within this book team was like learning a new dance. Although it wasn't always graceful, we were always surrounded by grace. Before Shannon even wrote the first word, we spent many hours on the phone, discussing the unique contribution our book could make, planning its organization, and sharing research information on a secured Web site. Throughout the months that she wrote and revised the chapters, team members provided suggestions and edits. We invited others—more than a hundred experts in different fields—to help us refine the chapters and give us new ideas for practical actions.

The book further benefited from Berrett-Koehler's collaborative approach, which offered us insights from their staff and reviewers.

Team Profiles

Shannon Daley-Harris, Writer

Serving as the writer for this book has been an immensely gratifying opportunity to tie together many threads of my professional and personal experience and commitments: from my early work teaching children with learning disabilities in Trenton, New Jersey, and tutoring in adult literacy and after-school programs in Belfast, Northern Ireland, to serving the Children's Defense Fund (CDF) as its director of religious affairs and, more recently, working as a strategic adviser, religious organizing consultant, and writer for CDF and other organizations addressing children's issues, poverty, and health care.

I've authored many publications on children's concerns (including *Welcome the Child: A Child Advocacy Guide for Churches* with Kathleen Guy; *A Child Advocate's Concordance to the Holy Bible*; *Holding Children in Prayer: An Advent Devotional,* and CDF's annual interfaith Children's Sabbath resource manual). I was thrilled by the opportunity to write a book that encompassed global issues and action. I am married to Sam Daley-Harris, founder of RESULTS, an international antihunger lobby, and executive director of the Microcredit Summit Campaign. Our children, Micah and Sophie, daily give me fresh glimpses into the wonder and the sacred worth of children and bring home the urgent, profound responsibility for working so that every child is nurtured and protected.

Jeffrey Keenan, Originator

First, I can't say enough about the incredible dedication, commitment, passion, and creative excellence of my book team colleagues—Shannon, Karen, Joy, and Jackie—and I am grateful that each of them agreed to be part of this project. As for my involvement, my motivation comes from my children, my faith, and my business experience.

My children are a constant reminder that, in an imperfect world, they are just as easily the ones who could end up in circumstances of hunger, homelessness, or other conditions of poverty—conditions that should never exist for any child. My Christian faith, as with most faiths of the world, compels me to take actions that will work for the good of others, especially those who may currently find themselves in circumstances of poverty. My twenty years of business experience, currently as strategic initiatives manager within Adobe Systems' Global Supply Chain Operations team, has provided a disciplined skill set and a rigorous approach to performance accountability, which I believe can be applied very pragmatically to the conditions, or root causes, of poverty in a way that can eliminate many (though not all) of the factors that contribute to its continued existence in the midst of a world with adequate resources and plentiful resourcefulness.

Karen Speerstra, Editor

When Joy called me one day in October 2005 and asked if I'd like to be a part of a book that would help end global poverty, I said "Yes!" without contemplating for a second the commitment, cost, energy, and resources necessary to tackle this mammoth task. Perhaps it was my twenty years in writing and book publishing that led me to so readily agree. I was, as the book team defined it, to help research, edit, help write on occasion, and generally "shepherdess" the project, particularly in "publishing matters." Working with these wonderful and totally dedicated, gifted people has been, without question, one of the most fulfilling projects with which I've ever been involved. My consulting company, Sophia Serve, is an editing and writing coaching service dedicated to helping people who are changing the world for the better, drawing on, as the name indicates, their innate Divine Wisdom. *Our Day to End Poverty* embodies that mission.

Criterion Ventures: Joy Anderson, Founder and President Jackie VanderBrug, Managing Director

Criterion Ventures is a national firm that incubates and scales social ventures that make for a better world. Criterion Ventures works with individuals and organizations that have a bold vision for what is possible for the world, and we partner with them to translate their vision into sustainable ventures. We saw offering this book, and the venture of creating it, as one more thread in the tapestry of ending poverty through reclaiming our connectedness. It has been our privilege to select and convene the team and manage the overall process of transforming the idea into reality. That process has connected and reconnected us with many organizations and individuals who are living their bold visions. They gave us hope, energy, and renewed commitment. We salute them.

The world is already connected. Invitations, such as those we issued to friends and acquaintances to contribute material for this book, make those connections visible. Among the amazing stories and visions we gathered, we found uncanny connections. We witnessed the web of relationships in connections such as these enable individual actions to leverage incredible impact. This is the stuff of social change.

About Berrett-Koehler Publishers

Berrett-Koehler is an independent publisher dedicated to an ambitious mission: *Creating a World that Works for All.*

We believe that to truly create a better world, action is needed at all levels—individual, organizational, and societal. At the individual level, our publications help people align their lives with their values and with their aspirations for a better world. At the organizational level, our publications promote progressive leadership and management practices, socially responsible approaches to business, and humane and effective organizations. At the societal level, our publications advance social and economic justice, shared prosperity, sustainability, and new solutions to national and global issues.

A major theme of our publications is "Opening Up New Space." They challenge conventional thinking, introduce new ideas, and foster positive change. Their common quest is changing the underlying beliefs, mindsets, and structures that keep generating the same cycles of problems, no matter who our leaders are or what improvement programs we adopt.

We strive to practice what we preach—to operate our publishing company in line with the ideas in our books. At the core of our approach is *stewardship,* which we define as a deep sense of responsibility to administer the company for the benefit of all of our "stakeholder" groups: authors, customers, employees, investors, service providers, and the communities and environment around us.

We are grateful to the thousands of readers, authors, and other friends of the company who consider themselves to be part of the "BK Community." We hope that you, too, will join us in our mission.

A BK Currents Book

This book is part of our BK Currents series. BK Currents books advance social and economic justice by exploring the critical intersections between business and society. Offering a unique combination of thoughtful analysis and progressive alternatives, BK Currents books promote positive change at the national and global levels. To find out more, visit www.bkcurrents.com.

Be Connected

Visit Our Web Site

Go to www.bkconnection.com to read exclusive previews and excerpts of new books, find detailed information on all Berrett-Koehler titles and authors, browse subject-area libraries of books, and get special discounts.

Subscribe to Our Free E-Newsletter

Be the first to hear about new publications, special discount offers, exclusive articles, news about bestsellers, and more! Get on the list for our free e-newsletter by going to www.bkconnection.com.

Get Quantity Discounts

Berrett-Koehler books are available at quantity discounts for orders of ten or more copies. Please call us toll-free at (800) 929-2929 or e-mail us at bkp.orders@aidcvt.com.

Host a Reading Group

For tips on how to form and carry on a book reading group in your workplace or community, see our Web site at www.bkconnection.com.

Join the BK Community

Thousands of readers of our books have become part of the "BK Community" by participating in events featuring our authors, reviewing draft manuscripts of forthcoming books, spreading the word about their favorite books, and supporting our publishing program in other ways. If you would like to join the BK Community, please contact us at bkcommunity@bkpub.com.